BRIDGE OF LOVE

What People Are Saying About *Bridge of Love*

Pam openly admits to having fear when sharing the Gospel, but through God's strength, she overcomes the fear instead of allowing fear to overcome her. *Bridge of Love* will give you some very practical "how-to" tips in evangelism. Pam's enthusiasm for reaching the lost is contagious and will excite you about your own opportunities.

— R. Larry Moyer
Founder and CEO EvanTell

I am a full-time evangelist who has preached the Gospel in all 50 states and foreign countries. Pam Walck's ability to incorporate the Gospel in daily interactions is without equal among any women I know! I highly recommend *Bridge of Love*.

— Dea Warford, Author
Evangelist: My Life Story, My Life Journey

I loved reading each chapter of *Bridge of Love*. It's very personal yet backed by Scripture. I love seeing how God has worked in Pam's life, taking the mess and changing it into a message! And, I love Pam's genuine love and care for the souls of others.

— Karen Roberts, Author
The Shunammite Woman: Restore What's Lost, Stolen. or Broken in Your Life

After reading *Bridge of Love*, I came to know who Pam is. I thought, "Wow, here is a person who loves Jesus Christ and has a passion of reaching out to lost souls."

— Mutinta Mwanyanda
Founder of Salvation and Healing Ministries for Orphans and Vulnerable children, feeding program, education, and clinic in Zambia, Africa

Anyone who knows Pam Walck will recognize how accurate and genuine these stories are. *Bridge of Love* treats success and failure, confirmation and uncertainty with the same open honesty. If you read this book you may find yourself sharing Jesus as openly as Pam does!

— Kevin Brown
President of TEACH and missionary trainer of pastors in the persecuted church

I highly recommend *Bridge of Love*, an inspiration for those who feel they are slightly lacking when it comes to talking to people about God and His love for all people. Pam shares the Truth: God will cause the seed to produce a full, bountiful harvest!

— Chris Lee
Author/film co-executive producer, Holy Spirit-filled member and prayer partner of The Fearless Storytellers' Movement

Overall, *Bridge of Love* is a practical, inspiring message for believers that encourages them to trust God, share the Gospel, and live genuinely according to His word.

— Paul Brown
Missionary, Entrepreneur, Marine Veteran

Bridge of Love offers a great treasure of examples of how God can work through us as we walk in faith and share His love with those around us. I have become bolder in my faith after reading these true accounts.

— Sharon Ana Entress
Researcher at the University of Buffalo

I loved reading *Bridge of Love*! It's so clear and direct and simple, that I couldn't put it down once I began!

— George Pulinthitta
Retired corporate banker

I enjoyed *Bridge of Love* very much. It contains powerful stories of sharing the Gospel with the people we meet along the way.

— Karen Haag, Author
Healed for His Glory: My Journey from Pain to Purpose

My favorite part of *Bridge of Love* is her ability to create such a simplistic second nature approach when sharing the Gospel, an endeavor, in my opinion, most Christian's are afraid or uncomfortable doing or even trying. A stress-free, easy, and inviting read!

— Jacqueline Lopez
Dental hygienist

BRIDGE OF LOVE

30 TRUE STORIES OF FAITH IN ACTION

PAMELA WALCK

Bridge of Love
by Pamela Walck

Copyright © 2022 Pamela Walck
Harbor Light Publishing

Cover and Interior Design: Kara Starcher
Author photographer: Shaun Smith

ISBN (paperback): 979-8-9871799-0-1
Library of Congress Control Number: 2022921973

31 30 29 28 27 26 25 24 23 22   1 2 3 4 5

Dedication

To my family who I love very much, my friends, and the patients I've had the privilege of working with over the years.

Contents

Hell Gate Bridge: Cover Photo

WHILE WRITING THIS MANUSCRIPT, I thought about the cover of my book nearly every day. I've always loved bridges. I remember going on a short trip to Pittsburgh, while I was in my 20's, mainly because they had so many bridges. Little did I know that years later, when I became a Christian, I would often use the bridge illustration to describe what happens when we trust in Jesus as our Savior—we are reconciled to the Father through faith alone in Christ and what He did for us. He's the bridge.

The cover designer for *Bridge of Love* wanted to know the specific style of bridge that I would like. I kept telling myself I needed to answer her, but life gets in the way sometimes. I "felt" like the Lord was telling me during prayer that my timing is not always His timing.

I decided instead of endlessly searching, which I had been doing—Googling images of bridges—I would just stop doing that and trust that God would show me somehow.

My mom loves watching the TV show "Judge Judy" which airs at 6:30 p.m. in New York. I walked into the living room one night at 6:10. Already preparing to watch her favorite show, Mom was mindlessly watching a program I can't stand. I said, "Lets

1

watch the news and see what's going on." I changed the channel and chatted with her aide while occasionally glancing at the TV.

I caught the last 15 seconds of a news story that showed a bridge in the background. "That's the one!" I blurted out. "That's the bridge I want for the cover of my book."

I thought the story was about something happening in New York City. I did a quick image search of New York City bridges. I saw it right away. There it was—Hell Gate Bridge.

How strange, I thought. What a name! Wow, is that from God or Satan? I looked up the history of the bridge. When I talked to my friend Ana later on the phone, she pointed out the history of the bridge. It's design had saved people from the treacherous waters below. Plus the bridge is red, just like the blood of Jesus who saves us from our sins when we repent and trust in Him.

Amazing . . .

CHAPTER 1

Love Requires Courage

HIS HAND FELT COLD. "DAD, wake up," I cried. I turned on the basement light. "Dad," I yelled a second time. He sat slumped in his chair, with one arm around the back of the chair, eye glasses down on his nose, and no response from him. A blood-curdling scream came out of my throat, "Mom, call the ambulance."

I found my father dead years ago. A decade later, my phone rang at home on a Friday night. My brother's son, Jay, spoke with a quivering voice. "Aunt Pam, my father's dead."

"What? I don't believe it!"

"They found his crashed car with him inside, upside down with a broken neck. I have a Niagara County Sheriff standing right here."

The Sheriff got on the phone with me and confirmed what my nephew had said. They had identified the man as my older brother, Donnie. Hospital doctors pronounced him dead on arrival.

I got off the phone, crying uncontrollably. "Why, God, why?" Tears streamed down my face. "Lord, please accept my brother into Heaven. I do not know whether Donnie believed in Jesus as his Savior."

In that moment, I felt the tender comfort of a God who promised to never leave nor forsake me. God didn't tell me where my brother ultimately ended up, of course, but He immediately reminded me that we cannot pray someone into Heaven after they're gone. Each person must decide to accept or reject Jesus while alive. God does not force Himself on anyone.

Both of these sudden deaths impacted my passion for sharing the Gospel. Through my work as a physical therapist, I often see people dying. Sometimes, a lingering illness makes their death long and drawn out. Others, like my dad and brother, die instantly, without warning.

After my father died, I thought about the effect of his passing on my own life and my mother's. I assumed my dad went to Heaven because I mistakenly thought everyone who went to church ended up there. His death prompted my searching. I checked out many books from the library and read about the white light, reincarnation, anything I could get my hands on about the after-life. I read everything except the Bible.

By the time my brother died, I had trusted in Jesus and understood from reading the Bible that "We are saved by grace, not works lest anyone should boast" (Ephesians 2:8–9). It doesn't matter what anyone did during their life—church attendance, baptism, confirmation. No person could earn his or her way into Heaven. The only thing that matters is whether we have repented and trusted in Jesus Christ.

I didn't know my brother's beliefs. Donnie had not attended church in a while; however, two months before his tragic death, I invited him to my church, and he went. Unfortunately, though I told him my story of how I came to trust in Jesus, we never had a conversation about his faith and whether he had trusted in Christ or not.

Many people avoid talking about faith out of fear or thinking that the conversation will take a controversial turn. But Jesus taught there's only one way to Heaven, and it's through Him (John 14:6). Because I've experienced the fragility of human life, I want as many people as possible to go to Heaven, not Hell.

Recently, I sat next to a couple on a plane. During the flight, I asked the man about his beliefs.

"I'm a back-slidin' Methodist," he said with a snicker.

His attitude made me wonder if he took Christianity seriously. I probed deeper. "What do you think of the Bible?"

"Well, I don't believe in the miracles."

"Who is Jesus Christ to you?" I asked.

"I think he's a good man."

"Only a good man?"

"Well, yeah, he did a lot of great things, but I don't think those were miracles."

"Do you believe Jesus rose from the dead?" I asked.

"No," he said.

His answers didn't surprise me. Though he'd been a man raised in the church, based on his responses to my questions, he remained an unbeliever.

We talked for awhile, and he seemed very scientifically minded. "If I can't see it, I don't believe it," he said.

"Did you see the Civil War?" I asked. "You weren't there for that, but we have historical records and testimonies that it took place. The fulfillment of Old Testament prophecies, along with all of the scientific and historical evidence, proves the Bible true and Jesus Christ is God."

At some point he seemed closed to further discussion. I encouraged him to read some books about the evidence for Jesus and also to read the Gospel of John, a little every day, and ask God to reveal Himself. We got off the plane and parted ways on friendly terms. I pray that God would use whatever seeds were planted in his mind during our conversation to move him to seek the Lord.

Left: Dad and Mom at dinner;
Right: My brother Donnie in his 20s. He loved being in the Navy.

When speaking to people about Christ, we may meet some resistance, and we need to let the Holy Spirit guide us as to when to speak and when to keep silent. I used to feel nervous when I'd ask a person about their relationship with Jesus, but it's not about me, it's about the individual and God. He can use us as tools through both our actions and conversations to bring people to Himself or to grow their faith.

Years ago, I went to a New Year's Eve celebration dinner at a church. After midnight, they had prayer. On my knees, I prayed fervently asking God to save my family and friends. In my heart, I clearly felt the words, "I can do all things through Christ who gives me strength" (Philippians 4:13). Prayer is critical, but we need to boldly share Christ with our words and actions. In the book of Acts, not one person came to Christ without first hearing the Word of God preached to them.

When my thoughts center on Christ and the Kingdom and another person's soul rather than my own, courage and love for others triumph over fear. I now enjoy sharing the Gospel. How could I not, knowing that perhaps someday I'll see in Heaven the people with whom I shared the Gospel or prayed for their salvation?

I no longer look at the Great Commission, "Therefore go and make disciples of all nations, baptizing them in the name of the Father and of the Son and of the Holy Spirit and teaching them to obey everything I have commanded you. And surely I am with you always, to the very end of the age" (Matthew 28:19-20) as something only pastors or missionaries do. As Christians, we have all received a call to share Jesus through words and deeds, no matter our ages or careers.

As I reflect on my father's and brother's deaths and my hope of seeing them again in eternity, I recognize that sometimes the most important questions remain unasked. If we don't ask a person about his or her relationship with Jesus, who will?

CHAPTER 2

I've Never Been Happier

"MY SHOULDER REALLY HURTS."

"Sorry to hear that, Mike. I'll be your physical therapist today since Bob is on vacation. Have you been doing your physical therapy exercises?"

"Yes, and my shoulder is moving better. I just have some pain today."

As I worked with Mike, I found out that he volunteered at the hospital I worked at. He counsels people heading into recovery from alcohol and/or drug addictions. Mike was in his late fifties with a mustache and gray hair pulled back in a pony-tail. He worked in construction, but he'd stopped a few months before due to the shoulder pain.

Mike noticed a bumper sticker on the back of my computer: "Exercise Daily Walk with the Lord." "That's an interesting sticker."

"I got it from a friend of mine, Jane, who passed away a year ago. It was on her wheelchair and I thought it was cool, just like her. She was really a dedicated Christian."

As I stretched his arm, I asked him about his volunteering. Mike told me how he'd been free from alcohol for several years now and how the 12-Step Program helps people with their addictions.

"What got you through the program?"

"Asking my higher power to stop the addiction."

"Your higher power? And who is that?"

"Well, to me, God."

"And who is God?"

"Someone who knows everything going on in my life and wants to help."

"Is He Jesus?"

"I guess so, I'm not really sure. I was raised in the church, but haven't gone in years."

After stretching and icing his arm, Mike seemed like he was just about to leave when a thought popped into my head. I quickly ran over to my desk and grabbed a CD. I kept a few in my desk, just in case I wanted to give one to someone.

"Mike, this is a CD of my pastor's story of his faith. It's pretty interesting. Would you like to listen to it? I'm giving this to you as a friend, not a therapist. And if you don't want it, you certainly don't have to take it."

"Sure, I'll listen to it. Thanks. See you in a few days."

I prayed Mike would listen to the CD and that the message it contained would draw him closer to Jesus. I know people who struggled with addictions and were able to conquer them with the 12-Step Program. God, however, isn't just a higher power; rather, He is the God of the universe—the Trinity that came to earth in flesh as Jesus.

Mike worked with his original therapist, Bob, at his next session, but he walked over to me during the appointment. I wondered what he wanted to say to me.

"Pam, that new exercise you gave me is helping. It's a good one. And…I listened to the CD twice, and cried both times. I gotta meet this dude Jerry!"

"You're welcome at my church anytime. Sunday services are at nine and eleven." I gave Mike general directions and told him I hoped to see him there.

The following Sunday before the 11:00 service, I spotted Mike in the coffee area.

He laughed heartily when he walked up to me. "Pam, when you said the name of the church was The Chapel, I pictured something small. This is a big church!" He waved his arms around the area he stood in.

"Well, you didn't ask how big it was."

I sat next to Mike at the service along with several other friends I introduced him to. Over the next few weeks Mike continued getting his physical therapy from my co-worker, Bob, but he made a point of letting me know that he was continuing to attend services at my church.

One Sunday, I saw Mike praying with one of the pastors in the fireside room. Mike later told me in the lobby that he had trusted in Jesus as his Savior. I was elated for him! Some of my friends and Mike went to lunch later, celebrating. It amazed me all that had transpired after our short initial conversation.

After Mike stopped his physical therapy and went back to work, I ran into him only at church, except for when he occasionally stopped in the physical therapy gym after volunteering to say hello to the therapists.

Within a year, Mike told me he had joined the choir and the worship arts team. He said a lot of changes were happening in his family. He stated several times, "I've never been happier." His daughter, Courtney who previously was not close to him, now talked to him daily even asking Mike for advice. After Mike invited Courtney to church for a year, she finally agreed there may be something to this, given the changes she has witnessed in Mike. Courtney has more and more accepted the existence of

Jesus, and she is actually interested when he tells her about the things he gets involved with or through the church.

Mike brought his granddaughter, Aubrey, Courtney's little girl, to the children's ministry, King's World on Sundays. Aubrey made an impact on Courtney and her husband as she excitedly discussed Noah and other characters from the Bible to them. Her exact words were, "there was this dude with a big boat with lots of animals cause it was raining."

"Pam, I felt like God was after me for awhile. Then you talked to me and gave me that CD. That's how I ended up finding Him."

As for myself, I'm just glad to see the ripple effect. We are to reproduce disciples for Jesus, and that's exactly what happened with Mike. "Therefore go and make disciples of all nations, baptizing them in the name of the Father and of the Son and of the Holy Spirit, and teaching them to obey everything I have commanded you. And surely I am with you always, to the very end of the age" (Matthew 28:19-20).

I felt overjoyed and grateful to God for working in Mike's life when I saw the changes that occurred since I first met him. Sometimes little things in life like conversations, or things we do or don't do, may not seem significant at the time. But added up they can make a difference. Whether it's exercising, giving to worthy causes, eating healthy, and especially sharing Christ—the choices we make can result in changes in our life or someone else's.

God used me in Mike's life in a small way and I praise Him for the privilege of seeing someone surrender their life to Christ. That's even better than helping a patient with their shoulder problem.

Note

After many years of Mike faithfully serving in the music ministry at my church, the leadership decided to make a big change, which ultimately decreased the number of people

Mike, me, and my cousin Sandy

needed. That meant Mike had no place in the music ministry. He took it very hard.

Whenever I saw Mike, he continued to talk about how upset he was about not being involved in music at our church. No matter how much I (and others) listened and encouraged Mike, he couldn't seem to accept their choice, so he decided to help somewhere else to use his talents. Ultimately, Mike left the church. He attended a different church for a little while, and I hoped he would get involved in music there, but he never continued.

Unbeknownst to me, Mike also went through several hardships in one year. When we talked on the phone a few times, I asked him how he was doing spiritually. He assured me he was okay and that he watched church online. Encouraging Mike to seek God and continue to look for a church or spend time with other Christians that we knew seemed fruitless.

Within a month after our last phone conversation, someone told me he was in the intensive care unit, on a ventilator, with jaundice from drinking. Shocked, I had no idea he had returned to alcohol; he seemed to have progressed so far away from his old lifestyle. I honestly forgot his past. Prior to my initially meeting Mike, he was involved with Alcoholics Anonymous, but he had not attended meetings in a long time.

Mike continued to decline physically. It was horrible for family and friends to see him so sick. His family stayed in his hospital room 24 hours a day.

A friend who worked at the hospital, stopped by Mike's room one day and led him to repent and rededicate his life to Jesus. Mike died shortly after that.

It's sad that Mike's life was shortened by alcohol addiction, but it's particularly heartbreaking that he did not reach out for help. Still, I'm thankful knowing that Mike knew Jesus, and I do believe I will see him in Heaven one day.

CHAPTER 3

In the Aisles of Walmart

As I drove down Niagara Falls Boulevard about ten o'clock on a Saturday night, I realized I needed some eye makeup, particularly mascara, for the next day. "I'll run into Walmart," I thought, "that won't take too long."

After walking into the store, I stood in the cosmetics aisle looking at products. So many mascara brands with different promises—Vitamin E, longer or fuller lashes, the list went on.

I stood there debating for fifteen minutes. "God," I thought, "I have a problem. Why can't I make a little decision over which mascara to get?"

"Go witness to them."

The inner voice startled me. It seemed like God just said that to me. I turned around not knowing what to expect. About 30 feet away stood two young women studying different perfumes. They had veils on their heads and wore long dark dresses. I presumed they were Muslims. So focused on finding mascara, I hadn't noticed anything or anyone around me. There could have been a fire in the store, and I probably wouldn't have seen it.

The women appeared to be in their late 20's. Even though I

could barely see their faces, they both had pretty features. They chatted and giggled to each other occasionally.

I silently prayed, "Lord, are you kidding? You want me to witness to two complete strangers?"

Silence.

I thought again about the prompting, "Witness to them."

I casually walked over to the perfume area where the two women stood smelling sprays from sample bottles of perfume. What should I say? How could I start a conversation with people I don't even know—especially a conversation about Jesus.

Ok, I thought, I'll make a quick decision. Whether that inspiration came from God or just my imagination—I decided to obey it. I do know God wants us to evangelize and bring Christ to the ends of the world—even in Walmart. It wouldn't hurt anyone, and it reflected God's heart for people.

The words came out of my mouth, "Where are you two from? You sound like you have an accent."

Both glanced at me and smiled. "We're from Turkey."

"Oh wow! Are you on vacation, or do you go to school here?"

The older appearing of the two women spoke. "We both go to college. My sister came to visit from Turkey, but she's leaving tomorrow. I attend the University at Buffalo."

"My name is Pam. Hi. And what are your names?"

"I'm Selva, and this is my sister, Nehir."

"What do you study in school?"

Selva, the one who lived here in Buffalo, said, "My husband and I take engineering at the University of Buffalo. We're both PhD candidates."

"I'm in my first year of medical school in Turkey." Nehir added.

The conversation continued for a few minutes, though nothing more than small talk about the Buffalo area and perfume.

How could I talk about Jesus? I thought.

"Can I ask you, those scarves you're wearing on your heads, do they represent something?"

"They are called hijabs—head coverings that we wear because of our Muslim faith."

"I see. I'm Christian. Have you ever gone to a Christian church service in the United States or Turkey?"

"A couple of times for weddings," Nehir said.

"How do you view Jesus?" I asked.

"We see Jesus as a prophet, a good teacher who lived on earth."

"You may know that Christians see Him differently. We believe Jesus is God. Have you ever read the Bible?"

"No, we study the Qur'an."

"Do you know then, that the Qur'an actually contains some important facts about Jesus?"

"Like what?" Selva asked.

"The Qur'an says that Mariam, who we would call Mary, a virgin, gave birth to Jesus. Christ lived a sinless life, pure, and holy, whereas Muhammad had a natural mother and father. The Qur'an also indicates that Muhammad had to have his heart purified and he asked for forgiveness of his sins."

"I'd have to see that in the Qur'an, I can't imagine it saying that," Selva commented.

"Christ raised the dead repeatedly—just like he can raise those who believe in Jesus as their Savior, upon their death."

We continued talking for 45 minutes. I knew the store would close soon, plus I felt pretty tired.

"Maybe we can get together and talk some other time. I could show you the references where you can see for yourself what we've been discussing. Would you like to exchange e-mail addresses?"

"Sure," Selva said.

Several weeks later, after e-mailing back and forth, I invited

Selva and her husband, Himmet, to my church, The Chapel at Crosspoint. They came. The service that day was different than usual. The entire morning was dedicated to the life of the current pastor who planned to retire. No sermon or invitation occurred, but the couple did get to meet a number of my welcoming friends and the pastor.

A few weeks after that, Selva and Himmet and I met several times at a local library on a Sunday afternoon to discuss Christianity and Islam. My friend Charity, a strong Christian with an engineering background, also came once. I thought they might relate to her well. We didn't get very far, unfortunately, as often our conversation turned into more of a debate. I send them e-mails occasionally, but I don't hear from them often. I ran into Himmet at the hospital where I used to work. He told me they had recently had a baby and were quite busy with school and the child.

Although at this point, though nothing came of our discussions, I know a seed was planted. I pray that God softens their hearts to hear and believe the truth.

That night in Walmart, I did purchase mascara, but I had a unique, wonderful experience, too—one that taught me some important life lessons. My plans don't always go as I want them to. Sometimes God interrupts them for His plans. God used my interests *and* my weaknesses to get me where He wanted me to go. I got my mascara, met some interesting people, and shared Jesus with them. Though Himmet and Selva don't know Him yet as Savior, I continue to pray they will one day.

CHAPTER 4

My Point of Surrender

SEVERAL YEARS AGO, ON A warm, afternoon with the sun bask-
ing its last rays on my arm through the open window of my car, I
drove to my church. After a long day at my job as a physical therapist, I could feel some soreness and aching in my lower back.
I tried to ignore it because of my time crunch. As I changed
into my outfit for *The Life of Christ* performance, a long robe and
sandals, every move I made sent twinges of pain up and down
my back and legs.

The following day I thought, what have I done to get myself
into this condition? I exercised several times a week for the past
ten years and as usual had gone to the gym that evening.

A friend spotted me barely moving around the facility and
came over. "Pam, what's wrong?"

"It's probably nothing," I said, "I'll be OK."

I went home to apply ice to my back, and tried to do some of
the exercises I knew. They did not help my condition.

The next few days I worked, but with much difficulty. The
pain in my back and legs felt unbearable. I knew I needed help
and finally walked down to our employee health department and
said, "That's it. I can't do this anymore. Something is wrong with

me." The medical personnel placed me on sick leave for several weeks while waiting to get authorization for an MRI.

My two-page MRI report appeared filled with descriptions of numerous problems. No one in the hospital who saw it could believe someone in their thirties would have so much wrong with her back. With four, small, herniated discs and several pinched nerves, the prognosis for my back healing quickly looked slim.

Back at home, when I could finally be weak and vulnerable, I cried out, "Why me?" After all the work I had gone through the past ten years; I graduated with an accounting degree, even passed the CPA exam, but I did not like the work. I went back to school again for another degree, this time for physical therapy. Could this be happening? All the years of striving away, only to result in not using what I learned?

I really liked my job because of the interactions with many patients and their families. I found it rewarding to see a patient, who could not move when they got admitted to the hospital, oftentimes regain the ability to walk by the time they left.

But given this news, it seemed like my career as a physical therapist could end. How could I return to treating patients with this extreme level of pain in my back and legs? I could walk no further than down my short driveway, a far cry from previously when I walked nearly eight hours a day and then regularly went to the gym after work.

No one thought my back would heal. Almost two months had gone by, and the intensity of pain had not changed. Even putting on my clothes each morning proved difficult. I had to throw my leg up into the air in order to get my pant leg over my foot. The doctors had advised me not to bend at the waist.

Lying on a floor for two months hardly moving felt unbearable, but that's what I had to do—an excruciating task for an active person. The living room floor's hard surface gave me some mild pain relief.

My discouragement grew. The exercises my physical therapy instructor and friend had given me did not help; neither did all the medications the doctor prescribed. The more upset I got over my lack of healing, the more pain I felt.

"God," I cried, "Where are you?" I did not understand why my back would not heal. How long could this go on?

Until one day I reached into my mailbox and pulled out a Christian magazine. In one of the articles, I read how Jesus has the power to heal. Jesus heals. What was I thinking? All this time I prayed to God with empty words. Until then, I had not really believed in my heart that God could heal me. I thought putting my faith in medical science and my own effort would help me get better.

I prayed and asked God to forgive me for not relying on Him. I asked him to forgive my lack of contentment these past months. Not until my point of surrender to His will did peace finally come. "For I have learned to be content whatever the circumstances" (Philippians 4:11).

If it was the Lord's will, He could heal me, and that is what I wanted. "Jesus," I cried, "please heal my back. Let me go back to work with my patients and let me walk again without pain. But if You decide not to, I will not lie here crying and discontent any longer, I will go on with my life the best I can. I know You will always love me."

God healed my back. Within a week, I went back to work pain-free. My regret came later over not telling others what He had done. My own pride kept me from saying that He had cured me. Not exercises, nor pills, nor anything else but the Lord had healed my back.

CHAPTER 5

Body, Mind, and Soul

AT ONE POINT DURING OUR relationship, my boyfriend suggested we live together. "I need to see if we'd get along because we're so different from each other." He looked at me squarely in the eyes.

I wanted to get married. We'd certainly dated long enough, but Ken had his doubts.

"Where will I sleep?" I asked him.

"I have two bedrooms. You can have one, and I'll sleep in the other."

"Wouldn't trying to see each other every other night give you the answers you want?" I responded as I squeezed his hand. "Why do we have to set up house?"

Shortly thereafter, my friend Chrissy counseled me about Ken and me living together. "If you live with a man, it doesn't show Christ-like qualities and would reflect badly on your Christian witness to the world. Basically, you'd look just like everyone else who doesn't follow God. Just because others—in this case millions of others—are doing something contrary to God's Word, does not make that something right."

I kept thinking about what Chrissy said. I knew that, even

if we slept in separate bedrooms, it would not look good to others. Everyone would assume we were sleeping together. Living together would also add temptation to our relationship.

In addition, what do all the statistics say? Those who live together before marriage have a much greater chance for divorce. I didn't want a bigger chance, but a lesser one. I also read that those couples who waited for physical intimacy until after they married had a much lower divorce rate because they committed to each other. Living together to me seemed like such a cop-out, as though someone said, "I'm not willing to marry you. So let's act as if we're married and if either one of us doesn't like something we can move on." Insinuating, no harm was done. Unfortunately that idea is false, for in every failed relationship, we leave a piece of our heart. We need to protect our heart and remember that God gave us all a conscience and the Bible to discern right from wrong.

Initially, I told Ken a firm no. But him constantly claiming confusion and insisting that our living together would determine our compatibility, wore away at me.

I finally said, "Maybe I would consider it."

That did it for him. The following week he bought new living room furniture so his place would feel like *our* place when I moved in.

It's funny how God orchestrates events. The next day, my friend Max, who lived in another state, called me. Max had lived with his girlfriend for the past few years.

We chatted for a few minutes before he mentioned, "I'm still not sure whether I want to marry her."

That night I wrote in my journal: "Don't live with a man!"

Ken and I broke up shortly after because of my unwillingness to live with him before marriage. Several months later, I received a call from him saying he had a change of heart. He understood my view because he had recently trusted in Christ as his Savior.

As a young believer myself, I thought Ken had already trusted in Christ—I reasoned wrong. If I lived with Ken or married him before his commitment to Christ, the relationship could have proved very difficult. I didn't know at that time, that the Bible says not to marry an unbeliever. "Do not be yoked together with unbelievers" (2 Corinthians 6:14). To yoke is to team together, whether through a marriage, strong friendship, or business partnership. In hindsight, I should have had conversations with Ken and asked him what he believed, instead of talking about my new found faith in Christ all the time.

God, however, knew my heart, and He changed Ken's during the hard process of breaking up. I may never have heard from him again, but if that happened, God had a different plan for me. I knew from my conversations with Ken that the courageous and righteous thing in God's eyes was to end that relationship.

If two people seek God faithfully, maintaining a healthy physical distance will only strengthen the upcoming marriage in the long run. Often two Christians will speed up the wedding date because they don't want to violate each other's purity. But if only one partner is willing to obey the Lord, as initially was the situation between Ken and me, it's a forecast for disaster.

A pastor's wife once told me, "The devil wants you in bed before marriage, and out of bed after."

Sometimes going against the norm in the world may seem difficult and unusual, but you need to expect that in living out the Christian life. "You were taught with regard to your former way of life, to put off your old self, which is being corrupted by its deceitful desires; to be made new in the attitude of your minds; and to put on the new self, created to be like God in true righteousness and holiness" (Ephesians 4:22-24).

We each need to decide whether to obey God or take much

of the current cultures' attitudes, all too frequently exemplified in our prime time television shows that espouse the mantra "if it feels good, why not?"

Noah prospered after taking a stand and building the Ark without a drop of rain in sight. His faith preserved his life and his family's lives while the rest of the world, who most likely mocked and ridiculed him, perished in the flood. The popular opinion of disbelief and unrighteous living resulted in their death.

Saying no to living together and sexual impurity, even if it angers or hurts the other person, demonstrates true love to yourself, and the other person. Even if the other person doesn't understand, God does, and He will bless you for it. "Keep away from sexual immorality. All other sins that people may commit are done outside the body; but the sexually immoral person sins against his own body. Do you not realize that your body is the temple of the Holy Spirit, who is in you and whom you received from God? You are not your own property, then; you have been bought at a price. So use your body for the glory of God" (1 Corinthians 6:18-20).

In my past, I made many mistakes with men and dating, but He can make my sins "as white as snow" (Isaiah 1:18). He can change me. God chose me, and I choose to honor Him with my heart, mind, body, and soul to think as Christ would. By faith, we need to make decisions and choose to love ourselves wisely.

CHAPTER 6

Baptism Following Belief

I GREW UP IN A traditional, church-going family. As a child and teenager, I knew on Sundays, or at least every other Sunday, my parents expected to go to the service. But I didn't know the Lord. I didn't know Jesus—until the age of 31.

As I read my Bible in the years after surrendering my entire self to Christ, I noticed many verses on baptism. Because my pastor baptized me when I was an infant, I frequently wondered why the Bible never mentioned baptism of babies. Because I wanted to know their view, I decided to e-mail the head of the denominational church I attended as a child. I asked, "Could you please provide Scriptural support for infant baptism?"

I received two verses in reply. "Let the little children come to me" (Matthew 19:14). This section of the Bible described purely how Jesus prayed for children—nothing mentioned about baptism. The other reference cited Acts 16:33, which describes how, after they were miraculously released from jail, Paul and Silas immediately went to the jailer's house. The jailer and his family asked what they needed to do to get saved. "After Paul and Silas preached the Word to them, they then believed and 'he and all his family were baptized.'" The representative from the denominational church told me that a baptism of a baby could have happened in the household.

In my opinion, these references cited by the man provided no evidence for infant baptism. All the other verses in the Bible—referenced something to this effect: they believed and were baptized. I looked up the reason for baptism in the Scriptures. It doesn't save someone. Christian baptism shows that a person has trusted in Jesus Christ as their Savior and is publicly declaring their faith. Believers get baptized out of obedience and their love for Jesus.

I decided the time had come for me to get baptized—really baptized as a believer. I'm sure my parents meant well, when they agreed to have their infants baptized. They loved us, and their church tradition performed baptism of babies. But traditions don't supersede the Bible, and, when you actually study the Word of God, you do not see baptisms of babies. An infant has no ability to decide if they believe in Jesus as their Savior and want to follow Him. The dedication of a baby—where the parents pledge to bring up their child in a Christian home, teaching the child about Jesus—seems very appropriate. But the individual must decide for themselves if they believe and get baptized—and only when they have the capacity to do so.

Pastor Rich George gave me the full body immersion of baptism at my church, The Chapel. I remember going into the water trembling and crying out of joy. (I can get somewhat emotional.) Years later, as I think back to that day, I'm so thankful for the commitment I made.

I'm very glad I know Jesus as my Savior, and I wanted to express it to the world. Just like in a marriage, the ceremony demonstrates in front of others the expression of your commitment to one another. It shows a willingness to surrender your will to another—in my case, to the God of the universe who already showed his love for me by dying on a cross more than 2,000 years ago. He showed His love through an action, and I wanted to show mine, too.

Like the brave believers of the early church, I hope I will always show love toward Him until I die and see Him in Heaven with the glorious reunion of the body of Christ.

"But when they believed Philip as he proclaimed the good news of the kingdom of God and the name of Jesus Christ, they were baptized, both men and women" (Acts 8:12).

CHAPTER 7

So You Want to Know the Future?

MIDNIGHT ABOUT TWO WEEKS BEFORE my October 31st birthday, and I felt utterly worn out. "Whew!" I had dragged from my basement to the curb years of accumulated Halloween articles—devils, witches, anything that resembled the occult.

Driving home from the mall several hours earlier, I tuned into a local Christian radio station. The announcer discussed Halloween and the occult. He said that, as Christians, we should not get involved in any aspect of it. I pulled my car over on Millersport Highway and turned into a church parking lot to listen more intently.

Wow, I thought, does the Bible really address topics such as fortune telling? I had no idea.

The radio preacher discussed the witch of Endor and Saul. Many verses cited in the Old and New Testament told about turning away from consulting mediums, sorcerers, astrology, or anything related to these.

"Do not turn to mediums or seek out spiritists, for you will be defiled by them. I am the LORD your God" (Leviticus 19:31). Other verses such as Isaiah 47:13-15, Isaiah 47:13-15, Acts 16:16-19, and Acts 19:18-20 also command us to stay away from the occult.

I definitely believed the Bible to be God's Word, which has

been proven over and over as valid and correct. Consider this, "All Scripture is useful for teaching, rebuking, correcting, and training in righteousness so that the man of God may be thoroughly equipped for every good work" (2 Timothy 3:16).

I needed to choose between following God or indulging my own desires—in this case, that of keeping and displaying decorations that reflected something contrary to Him and His Word.

I felt convicted about my past behavior. In high school, I had written a monthly horoscope column, just made up, of course. Later, I got involved in tarot card readings, the Ouija board, and regular trips to Lily Dale (a town in New York known for mediums).

When I finally got home from my drive that night, I started ripping apart the basement. Since my birthday is on Halloween, I dressed up in costume—both for work, where I visited the patients' rooms, and for parties after work. Not a year had gone by when I didn't come up with some outlandish outfit. Most of my Halloween getups such as Little Boo Beep and the Energizer Bunny, were innocent enough costumes. But I had also dressed up as a vampire and a she-devil.

While in the basement, I came across other occult materials I'd collected over the years. All the time I was involved with these things, I desired to know the future and what to do with some aspect of my life.

That night, while listening to the radio program, I realized that I had not trusted God with my future. The truth was, I had shown a lack of faith. The Lord has the answers for everything, and He freely gives me wisdom—with the condition that I must listen to Him. I won't be able to discern His will through mediums and other crazy ways, but only through the Bible, godly counsel, and prayer. As I meditate on Scripture today, I find answers to many of my problems or questions in life.

For instance, I started reading the Bible initially because I wanted to know who to marry. God showed me the description of the character of the man I would want as my husband—kind, patient, not proud—admitting his weaknesses, loving, not rude (as my personality had poorly shown for so many years). You've probably heard a pastor read this list of qualities from 1 Corinthians 13 at a wedding.

What else did God reveal to me that I should desire in a mate? Someone who follows the Lord and wants His will for their life. Lastly, I wanted someone I would enjoy spending time with. Did the Bible say that? I don't think so, but it does talk about contentment and our desire for marriage to one person such that you never want to leave each other. Such a commitment is similar to what God says, "I will never leave you nor forsake you" (Hebrews 13:5).

My past history of relationships with men focused almost exclusively on their outside, their external qualities. After spending time with someone, you see how the insides of a person matter even more.

You don't want them to leave you or you them. That kind of love is so hard to find that Proverbs 31 calls it rare. A love for each other combined with excellent godly character is virtually impossible, except that He is the God of the impossible. With His hands on our lives to control circumstances and events, He allows us the potential to meet a person like that. All the while, He's working on us and our insides for at least two reasons—one, so we recognize the person He brings to us, and, two, so we change into the likeness of Him—Jesus.

That night—both the radio pastor's counsel and my purging of the basement—resulted in a desire to please Him more than I ever had. I wanted to obey God and tell others about His greatness and testify about everything He had done in my life.

After throwing out the items from the basement, I turned on the television and sat down. Kirk Cameron was speaking. I didn't know at the time that Kirk, star of the sitcom *Growing Pains*, had turned Christian evangelist. I listened closely as Kirk talked about winning souls for Christ and how to go about doing that. Swinging conversations from the natural to the spiritual and finding out what people believe. I wanted to be like Kirk Cameron, I thought, doing more for God, not for me. That night I realized the call God had on my life—to help transform hearts and souls through the Word of God, one at a time.

He truly does know the path we are to take. "Trust in the Lord with all your heart and lean not on your own understanding; in all your ways submit to Him and He shall direct your path" (Proverbs 3:5-6). Knowing this made me choose to want to obey, because I know He loves me and knows what's best for His sheep.

CHAPTER 8

The Keyboard

GIVE AWAY MY KEYBOARD—ARE YOU kidding me? That's a pretty expensive item, definitely in the thousand dollar range. An hour earlier, I looked around my spare bedroom, and my eyes came to rest on the keyboard. Looking at it, I felt inspired— almost God-driven to give the musical instrument to Emily. I felt some fear. That's a bold move, I thought, even operating in faith, as I barely knew her.

Still a fairly new Christian, I attended my church's weekly Bible study for singles. I had met Emily at the previous Saturday night's coffeehouse. I joined a few friends for fun, and hoping to meet some new people. After I walked in, I saw a woman about nineteen, tall and slender with light brown hair, sitting off to the side. She held a guitar. Later that evening she played a solo for us.

What an amazing night—listening to Emily play the guitar, sing, and share her story. At eighteen years of age she had just graduated from high school in Lancaster, New York, and had been offered a college music scholarship. As she rode the train, one afternoon, ready to embark on her new adventure, a thought suddenly hit her: I never asked God what He wanted for me. I've only pursued what I want to do. Emily didn't have a peace about this being the path God had chosen for her so she gave up the scholarship.

After prayer and searching, Emily ended up going to Ghana in West Africa to study at a Christian music school. She had returned to the Buffalo area on a school break to visit her family, and that's when I met her that evening at the coffeehouse.

As I sat listening to Emily, my tears flowed like a river. Wow, I thought, she is really pursuing Jesus. I was so impressed by her faith and humility. I wished I had that kind of deep relationship with the Lord. I kept putting my hand over my eyes to hide my tears. I felt embarrassed and surprised by the many joy-filled emotions I had as I realized the value of her wisdom in being true to Jesus and not her self-interests.

I knew Emily wasn't planning to leave town for another week, so my friend Laurie and I went to see her at another coffeehouse in Buffalo a few days later. This time, her mother accompanied her playing the drums. Same thing, tears flowed from me, as I listened to her gift of praise and worship and love for the Lord.

Now, as I sat in my apartment staring at the keyboard, I thought, it is scary to give something so expensive away. But why not? I don't use the instrument anymore. I took lessons for three months from my sister-in-law, Terry, who taught piano, but I just didn't like it enough.

During the time she taught me, Terry complimented my natural ability. She told me that, if I stuck with the piano, I would probably learn to play it well. It took a lot of practice, as does anything we learn that's new. Now, older and with less free time, I wanted to use those hours in a different way—going to the gym, visiting friends, volunteering. Had I taken lessons at a younger age, perhaps then I would have had the motivation to learn the instrument.

I stopped the lessons and actually felt a sense of relief, as though

I'd made the right decision. But now the keyboard sat in my second bedroom with a blanket covering it for more than a year.

After hearing Emily's riveting story at the coffeehouse event, I called her the next day to ask if she could stop by my apartment. I told her I wanted to make a small donation toward her education in Africa. That to me alone seemed a leap in faith for me—as I had never wanted to donate money to anyone like this. She had mentioned at the coffeehouse that both she and the school needed funds.

I reached for the telephone to call her a second time. "Emily, are you possibly interested in a keyboard for you or the school in Africa?"

"Sure, we could always use one—as long as I can get it on the plane!"

Later, she came bouncing in the door with a big smile on her face—in stark contract to the rainy, murky weather outside. By the time she came over, I had found the original box for the keyboard in my basement.

"That's a great keyboard." She ran her fingers over the smooth keys and flashed me another grin. "I'll manage to get it to Ghana somehow."

Emily and I communicated sporadically via email over the next ten years. I even took it upon myself to sell thirty copies of her CD, *Playtime,* at my job and elsewhere to help promote her music. Many people loved her voice, the African music, and the lyrics. I know I did.

Once in while I thought about the keyboard and wondered what happened to it. I just hoped Emily had put it to good use. I thought God prompted me to move into action by giving it to her, but I didn't know for sure. The situation seemed to make sense, so I stepped out in faith.

A few months later, when my former boyfriend, Ken, who had

given the keyboard as a present, found out that I donated it to an African school, he wasn't happy at all. But the keyboard belonged to me; he'd given it to me to use as I saw fit. I didn't expect him to understand when I gave it away. We had grown apart, and he didn't seem to care about Christ's will for his life then.

Ten years after I had given the keyboard away, I received a very unusual email from someone I didn't know. A man from the School of Worship (YWAM) in Ghana, Reverend Nicholas Oddoye, told me the keyboard had finally worn out. He thanked me for the donating it to their music school and shared how God has used it for ministry. I listened to his story—in awe that he had contacted me—until I realized Emily gave Nicholas my email address.

Tears welled up in my eyes. I had given away that keyboard ten years ago! And for all those years students had had the ability to use it, much more than I ever would have.

It's amazing how God used something like my own inspiration to choose to help others for His glory. And even though I may never have found out the results of my actions until Heaven, it inspired me to live even more by faith. "But store up for yourselves treasures in Heaven, where moths and vermin do not destroy, and where thieves do not break in and steal" (Matthew 6:20–21).

Emily R. Skinner now goes by Adjoa Skinner (Webb)—her Ghanaian name.

CHAPTER 9

The Paper That Never Ran Out

I'LL NEVER FORGET WHEN I packed to go to seminary. I decided to go to Dallas Theological Seminary to study the Bible so I could work in ministry one day, and share Christ's teachings more. I threw things out, gave away unwanted items, sold possessions, and rearranged the last of what I owned until finally I had only the things I planned to take with me to Dallas. Then I saw the stack of paper my mom had given me—11x17 pages that she said I could cut down to normal size. My sweet mom is resourceful!

As I looked down at the mildly-discolored paper, I thought of my dad. I found the paper in his desk. He passed away years ago, and my mom did not want to get rid of most of its contents. The drawers of his desk are still filled with all sorts of interesting articles from politics to fishing, as well as many of the hundreds of jokes he told throughout his life.

Looking at the paper my mom had given me also made me reflect on my move to Dallas. I knew I'd miss my family, friends, church, co-workers, and physical therapy patients. The hardest part was knowing I wouldn't see them for awhile. I planned on leaving the safety and familiarity of 37 years with family and friends to embark on the adventure of a lifetime.

I based my commitment to go to seminary on faith, but sometimes feelings of fear arose. Although I had traveled quite a bit throughout my life, I never lived more than 30 miles from where I grew up. Now I intended to move 1,400 miles away. Throughout the move, I thought of the Lord's promise, "I will never leave nor forsake you" (Joshua 1:5).

As I flipped through the sheets of 11x17 paper, I wondered about finances and felt my apprehension beginning to mount. At that time the words "I will supply all your needs" (Philippians 4:9) were impressed upon my heart. I sensed I would not even need to use this yellowing paper. I knew God provided for our needs, but computer paper seemed a stretch. Yeah right, God, I thought, you're going to give me paper. How is that possible?

After arriving in Texas and settling into seminary, I began writing lots of term papers. Once in awhile I'd glance at the dwindling paper supply by my computer and remember those words, "I will supply all your needs."

"You haven't given me paper yet God," I'd think.

Almost a whole year had gone by, and one hot July afternoon I walked into OfficeMax to purchase a new ink cartridge for my printer. Since I only had a small amount of paper left, I figured the time had now come to buy some. Disappointed, I remembered thinking again, "God, You never gave me any paper." The current sale indicated if I bought two printer cartridges, I would get two packs of paper free. That's nice, but it still didn't seem to fit the promise I felt the Lord had given me.

My ears perked up in the checkout line when the cashier said, "You know, anytime you bring in an old ink cartridge for recycling, we give you free paper."

"What?" I couldn't contain my surprise. "I've been coming to this chain of stores for years, and no one's ever told me that."

I walked out to the parking lot with tears of amazement. The

Lord does supply all my needs—in His time, and in His way.

Now, looking back, I regret doubting God's provisions, even in the small matter of computer paper. Although God meets our needs in different ways, He always proves Himself a faithful Father. The most important gift I received that day in the Office-Max store was not free paper, but the reminder that God's grace and love never fail. That reminder gave me greater faith to believe "With God all things are possible" (Matthew 19:26).

CHAPTER 10

The Walgreens Parking Lot

"Can I wash your windows for a dollar?"

Oh boy, I thought. It figures somebody comes up to me today. All morning I felt discouraged. I couldn't help but dwell on my present circumstances—life seemed overwhelming with so much to do, difficulties with family and a relationship, and I often felt incredibly lonely. When I finally managed to leave my apartment and head to seminary, I stopped at a Walgreens Drug Store on the way. As I walked towards the entrance of the store, an unshaven man about 45 years of age approached me from the parking lot.

"Ma'am," I heard him say. I turned around and faced him. He had dirt on his tan pants and jacket, and a spray bottle of window washer fluid in his hand that matched his blue eyes.

"Yeah, go ahead," I nodded toward my car then turned and hurried into the store.

As I quickly purchased a few things, I thought about the man outside. At least he's industrious. He didn't just ask for money; he wants to work for it.

Outside I found him drying my windows with a newspaper.

"What are you doing?" I cried out. "Won't that scratch the windows?"

"No, newspapers work great on windows. I used to work for auto shops."

"Are you sure?"

"Yes." He worked fast to finish the job.

As I chatted with him, I kept my finger on the car alarm button the entire time. I found out his name—Billy Ray.

"How did you end up washing windows in a Walgreens parking lot?" I asked.

"I lost my job, and now I don't have a car."

"Can't you take a bus?"

"Yeah, but I'm late a lot and I get fired."

I wondered if he had an alcohol addiction. He did smell, but that could come from not washing his clothes.

"You've got a problem with your wiper blade. See here?" He showed me how the driver's side blade had split and could soon scratch my window.

I thought back to the last car I owned. I had scratched the window with a broken wiper blade resulting in over $600 in window damage.

"Wow, thanks for showing me that. I noticed it coming apart for the past few weeks, but for some reason ignored it."

"I can change the wiper blade for you," he said. "I'll walk over to the auto store across the street, if you want to drive over and meet me there?"

I considered it. Certainly, I did not want to put myself in any danger. But at 1:00 in the afternoon with people everywhere, I felt relatively safe. "OK."

I parked near the front door of the auto store. Inside, it appeared the people behind the counter knew Billy Ray.

As he changed the blade, we talked some more.

"Do you have a church you can go to?" I asked.

"Sometimes I go." He took a coin out of his pocket to show

me. It had a picture of Jesus on it. "I pray every morning to get through the day."

After I paid him, we talked more about his relationship with Jesus. Suddenly I realized how late it had gotten, and I started to leave.

"If you need any more car work, you can find me at Walgreens. I do oil changes, too."

"Thanks for your help, Billy Ray."

My mood had changed significantly once I stopped dwelling on my own problems and thought about someone else's needs. The rest of the drive to seminary, I prayed for Billy Ray. "Lord, help this man get a job and anything else he needs. If he has any addictions that are keeping him in this lifestyle, walk with him toward freedom. In Jesus' name, Amen."

The Lord amazes me in how He meets our needs—a person in need of work, and me, wiper blades.

CHAPTER 11

The Light Went On

As I PARKED MY SUV, behind the church, I glanced down at my dashboard. Oh no, a light is on. My mind quickly thought—service appointment.

I had recently moved to Texas to attend Dallas Theological Seminary, and I'd been visiting a local church for a few months. Normally I went on Sundays, but upon the recommendation of a member I thought I'd check out their Saturday evening service.

I quickly restarted the engine. How obvious—I never noticed the door ajar light shone when I opened it. How many college degrees do I have?

As I sat in the church parking lot about to get out again, I felt a strong need to pray. "Lord, lead me to sit where you want me to, next to someone you want me to meet." I'd never prayed those words before, but not knowing many people at the church yet, it felt a little lonesome sitting by myself.

I walked into the church and scanned the sanctuary. Hmmm, where should I sit? Looking down the long rows, I spotted a woman sitting near an end. I'll sit by her. She gave me a funny look as I settled into a seat near hers.

A few minutes later I realized the reason for her strange look. She got up and left with some people who evidently wanted to sit in that area.

Now what? Sitting alone again. I knew the Holy Spirit resided in me, but I thought of my prayer outside. If no one decided to sit next to me, why had I felt such a strong impression to pray that prayer?

After the service began, I saw a woman, about forty years old, walk up the aisle flailing her arms, frantically scanning the seats. She appeared mentally disabled.

The lady stopped right in front of me and said, "I can't find my sister. Where am I going to sit? Can I sit with you?"

"Sure." I motioned to the seat next to me.

Her face lit up and she gave me a big grin as she threw herself down into the seat.

"I can't see. Can we move up front?" she said loudly. The woman in front of us turned around.

"No, I'd like to stay here. Look, why don't you sit on the other side of me?"

She moved to the seat on my left and gave me another huge grin, from ear to ear.

"What if I can't find my sister, what am I going to do? I'm not supposed to sit alone."

"You'll be fine." I nodded at her.

She looked over as if to say thanks for taking care of me, helping me.

As the worship music continued, I watched her lift her arms clapping and waving. What a joy to watch her! Although we sat near the back of the church, I assumed neither her sister nor anyone could miss this woman's enthusiasm for God.

Once in awhile I'd see some tears in her eyes, but you could tell they were out of love. Watching her, my eyes filled with

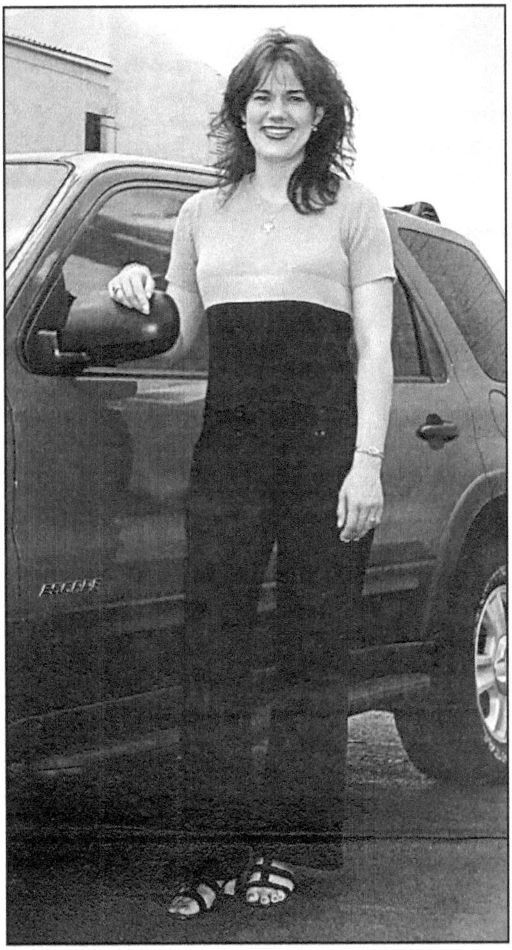

A photo from a newspaper with the caption: A mistaken engine light in Pamela's SUV led her to stop and pray before a Saturday evening service.

tears—the joy of seeing someone so grateful worshiping God in the House of the Lord.

"They took me up front." She pointed to the prayer rail. "They prayed for me, you know, the Pastor did."

"That's great!" I said.

After my seatmate made a few more comments, the woman in front of us turned around again.

I felt compelled to shush my new friend, as the woman

appeared irritated by our talking. I couldn't help but get a kick out of her—her faith-filled worship and abandon.

The minister began his Scripture readings. "Do you want to see the Bible?" I placed mine on my left thigh to share with her.

"I can't really read the Bible. My sister reads it for me."

"I'll show you." I opened to the passages and put my finger on each word. She seemed to follow along with her eyes.

After the service ended, I asked, "What is your name?"

"My name is Lucinda Lishka, but you can call me Lucy, or Inda."

"It's nice to meet you Lucinda." I gave her a broad smile.

Together, we walked down toward the front of the church, looking for her sister.

"What if I can't find her?"

"Don't worry Lucinda. She's here, and we'll find her."

A few minutes later Lucinda introduced me to her sister Melissa. They both thanked me, and Lucinda beamed another big grin.

"No, thank *you*," I told them both. "It was great sitting with you tonight, Lucy."

As I got back into my vehicle to drive home, the dashboard light went on again. I couldn't help but think about how God had not failed me. I met a woman in need of a friend—at a time when I needed one, too. The Lord faithfully answered my prayer by sending me to the seat where He wanted me—a prayer that might not have taken place if the light had not blinked in the first place.

CHAPTER 12

A Texas New Year's

MY FIRST NEW YEAR'S EVE in Dallas, Texas—I didn't know what to do for fun that night until I received an invitation a few weeks before the date.

"A house dance party? I've never heard of one of those. Texas has some unique get-togethers."

"Craig's got a sound system and dance floor in his living room. We'll have fun," my friend Heather assured me.

New Year's Eve finally arrived. Though I wasn't really sure what to wear to a dance party in a residential home, I managed to pick out a nice outfit, including a black skirt that would fan out if I spun around. After arriving at the party with a few friends, I walked into the house and saw a hardwood dance floor in the living room along with a large disco ball hanging from the ceiling.

I met many new friends that evening. About ten o'clock a tall, distinctive looking man with bright blue eyes wearing a grey suit walked in. He arrived with a shorter man with dark skin and glasses. I thought possibly he might be of Indian descent. They both looked about thirty-five years old.

"This is Roy and Muthu," someone said, as I was introduced to them.

"How do you two know each other?" I asked Muthu, the darker-skinned man.

"Friends from work," he said between bites of a piece of cake.

I found out that Roy, the taller man in the suit, used to attend Hillcrest Church, as had many of the people at the party.

I immediately wondered about Muthu's faith. Less than 3% of India's population is Christian. Did he attend Hillcrest Church or any church? "God," I prayed, "give me the words to say to Muthu so I can find out if he is a Christian."

As the evening progressed, people danced anything from swing to ballroom to freestyle. Roy appeared to be an experienced dancer, as he floated around the room with my friend Heather on his arm. They both laughed and smiled and made their dancing look so easy.

After midnight, with my thoughts still on having a potential conversation with Muthu, I walked through the main hallway and met up with him. Now's my chance I thought.

"So you work with Roy?"

"Yes, we're computer programmers," Muthu said with a distinct accent.

"Where are you from?"

"India, but I've lived in the United States for about three years." Muthu talked a little about his job at the bank where he and Roy worked. They had cubicles near one another and both went out dancing after work occasionally.

"Do you go to Hillcrest Church?" I asked.

"No," he replied curtly.

"What church do you go to?" I asked him in a friendly tone.

"Well, actually," he hesitated, "I'm Hindu."

"As a Hindu, what do you believe in?"

"Hindus believe in multiple gods, and that is my family's tradition. I actually don't believe in any god."

We continued to speak until after three in the morning,

Me, Muthu, and Ted at the Maid of the Mist, Niagara Falls, New York

comparing Muthu's beliefs with those of Christianity. Two other women from the party, Jennifer and Melissa, eventually joined the conversation as well.

"What do you think happens when you die?"

"It's like we fall asleep."

"That's a pretty sad state," I pursed my lips and slowly shook my head. "If that's the case, then what is our point for living then?" I took a sip of ice water.

"I don't know," he said. "You lead a good life and treat people well."

"Wow, there's got to be more to our existence than that. Don't you think we must have some purpose for living beyond now?"

He didn't have an answer for me.

Over the next several months, Muthu and I talked periodically on the phone, at social events, and through e-mail. I encouraged him to read the Bible, and he eventually read two books of the New Testament. Occasionally, I'd get a glimpse of God working on him. At an event we both attended, The Road Adventure, in an emotional moment Muthu said a song reminded him of Heaven. My eyes filled with tears.

God used Muthu, an unbeliever, to uncover some of my own problems. One night, I got home from work after a pretty distressing day. I was lying down on my bed upset about what happened with a patient. But then, Muthu called to discuss something he'd read in the Bible. Of all the days for him to phone me, I thought. I didn't feel like talking to anybody then, but I especially didn't want a heavy discussion about the Bible.

I answered the phone reluctantly. "Ok, Muthu, "I'm not feeling so hot, but what do you want to talk about?" Even as I spoke, I realized that despite my sad feelings, because I cared about Muthu and his salvation, I would be willing to talk.

"What's the matter, Pam?"

My tears started flowing. "One of my patients at work died today. It makes me feel horrible because, based on several conversations, I don't know if he ever trusted in Christ as his Savior. He died so suddenly. I'm also upset about other things—my health, my career, and my personal life."

"You worry a lot, don't you?"

"Well, yes, but most people do. And I have a right, there's a lot going on in my life, and I wish some things were different."

"Pam, what does it say right here in the book of Matthew? 'So do not worry, saying, "What shall we eat?" or "What shall we drink?" or "What shall we wear?"

For the pagans run after all these things, and your Heavenly Father knows that you need them. But seek first the kingdom and his righteousness, and all these things will be given to you as well. Therefore do not worry about tomorrow, for tomorrow will worry about itself. Each day has enough trouble of its own."'

My mouth dropped. I felt astounded by my own ignorance. Muthu quoted me a section out of the book of Matthew in the New Testament. He appealed to me using his intelligence and the Bible. God spoke His Word to me through an unbeliever.

Muthu and I now live in different countries, but we continue to keep in touch. "I pray for you all the time Muthu," I tell him. "I know Jesus wants you to believe in Him as Lord and have your sins forgiven."

I pray that one day Muthu will trust in Christ, just as I need to always trust in God's provision for my life and giving my troubles to Him.

CHAPTER 13

Two Stubborn People

A BURLY MAN IN HIS early 60's, a Vietnam Veteran with purple hearts, Mike resided in the apartment building next to mine. He originally moved to Dallas from the New York City area. I'd frequently see him walking around the complex—first with a cane and months later using a four-wheeled walker. Eventually his body declined and he went into a wheelchair.

When Mike got his dog, a beautiful golden retriever named Sniffles, I immediately bonded to the pair. It seemed as though everyone in Dallas had a dog except me.

"Mike, can I borrow your dog?" Sniffles soon became my adopt-a-dog. I'd take Sniffles for runs and long walks with him, which Mike couldn't do.

As Mike and I got to know each other better, I'd say, "Come to church with me Mike."

"Pam, I don't want to go," he'd respond.

"Oh come on, Mike; you'll meet lots of people and enjoy it. We can go to lunch after."

He went with me a few times—but never upon his initiation, always mine.

A tough cookie, Mike was a non-believing Reform Jew, and

Mike and his dog Sniffles

he happened to get me, an avid Christian evangelist, as a neighbor and friend.

"Pam, you're just like Clyde who tried and tried to tell me about Jesus. Clyde would do anything for me. Just before Clyde died, he promised that one day he'd send an angel to talk to me so I would believe. You're like a second Clyde."

"Well, I'm not an angel, Mike, but I do, like Clyde, want you to believe in Jesus."

I wouldn't give up on Mike. Sometimes I'd pray earnestly for him three times a day.

Then Roy came into my life. I met this handsome computer analyst at a New Year's Eve party. Over a year later Roy called me out of the blue and invited me to go swing dancing. I agreed. I enjoyed myself immensely that evening. A week later Roy asked me if I wanted to get dessert, and I again said yes.

As Roy was en route to pick me up, I finished ironing my clothes and a thought popped into my head. Roy might make a strong witness for my neighbor Mike. Roy had trusted in Jesus about ten years prior; he now attended Baruch HaShem Messianic Synagogue in Dallas.

"Let's invite my neighbor Mike to go out with us," I suggested to Roy when he arrived at my apartment. Roy, a friendly guy who had no problem meeting new people, readily agreed. I explained to Roy how I'd been talking to Mike for quite some time about Jesus, but thus far Mike's beliefs had not changed.

That night over coffee and laughs, Roy told Mike a little of the story behind his acceptance of Jesus. "I never really knew what love was," Roy said, "until Jesus came into my life. My family didn't like that I changed to Messianic Jewish. Actually, they still don't, but they've accepted it. Now, I'm a much nicer, kinder person, and they like that." Mike listened intently, but he didn't say much in response to Roy's story.

Over the course of the next year, Mike and Roy hung out together. Roy took him on Saturdays to Baruch HaShem. There he heard the incorporation of both Jewish customs and the Christian message.

Mike would still say to me, "Pam I love you as a friend, but I will never, ever become a Christian."

"Mike you can still be a Jew, but you'd be a Jewish Christian if you trust in Him. You'd have it all. Jesus was a Jew. He came for everyone—people of Jewish descent like you, Mike, and the Gentiles, like me, and most rejected Him. When you trust in Jesus as Savior, He will forgive your sins. It's a free gift. You don't have to do anything but have faith. The Bible says that,'If you declare with your mouth, "Jesus is Lord," and believe in your heart that God raised Him from the dead, you will be saved.'"

"Pam, I like the people at Baruch HaShem, they're friendly, but I'm never going to be a Christian, so don't bother trying to convert me."

But I wouldn't stop. I continued to pray for God to open his eyes to the fact that Jesus is our Lord—not just a teacher, or a prophet, or a good man. Mike met more and more friends who embraced Jesus as the Messiah, both at the Synagogue and at the Veteran's Hospital where he volunteered.

My family and others would tell me, "You can't get people to change."

I shut down the naysayers with a wave of my hand. "But God can, if they're willing, and often He uses others to help."

I couldn't deny it, at times I felt frustrated, very frustrated. "God, I don't know what else I can do. I've prayed for Mike constantly, invited him to church, Roy has done tons to try to influence him, and many, many people have witnessed to him about Jesus and shown genuine Christian love. What is it going to take? Please change his heart. I'm thinking of moving back to Buffalo and I'd really like Mike to trust in You before I leave."

On the weekend of Super Bowl Sunday, Mike and I took a three-day course, The Road Adventure. At the end of the third day, I walked out to my car to listen to the final scores of the football game.

Since I sometimes drove him home, I told Mike, I'd be right back.

I sat in the car with the seat reclined for about twenty minutes listening to the end of the game. When I walked back into the conference hall, I saw Mike hugging three women. His body looked shaky, but whatever happened seemed positive.

I touched his upper back, "Mike, what's going on?"

He cast me a nervous glance and spoke in his usual deep, gruff voice. "I'm not telling you."

"Mike, what happened?" I got down on one knee so I would be at his level in his wheelchair and looked into his eyes, "Why are you hugging these women?"

Sheepishly, he said, "I trusted in Jesus."

My jaw nearly dropped, "What? You did? Why didn't you want to tell me? That's so great!"

"I didn't want to tell you because you've been bugging me for so long. It felt like a bolt of lightning shot through me when I prayed to trust in Jesus."

"How did it happen?"

"Rob," he said.

Rob, a missionary and veteran, was one of the leaders at the

Me with Mike

conference. He and Mike seemed to hit it off from the beginning of the event.

I tore into the other room to search for Rob. I found him standing behind a conference table packing up his papers.

"Rob, what happened with Mike?"

Rob had a more reserved personality than mine. "I felt the Holy Spirit telling me throughout the weekend not to push Mike too hard. He was right on the edge of making a decision to accept Christ, so I didn't want to get him angry. At the end of the evening tonight, I asked Mike if I could pray for him. He said yes. As I prayed for him, Mike asked how he could trust in Jesus. So we prayed together, and Mike asked for forgiveness of his sins and trusted in Jesus as his Savior."

"That's amazing! Thank you, Rob. I'm so glad that you met Mike and this happened."

"It's all God's plan, and His timing. Mike was ready."

Rob later told me more of what happened over the weekend with Mike: "Mike could not deny the power of Jesus that flowed throughout the weekend in the lives of others," Rob said. "There was one drill in particular where we sort of guide participants through a visualization of Heaven. I had the privilege of walking Mike through it. Knowing Mike was Jewish, I used Jewish names (Yeshua, for example, for Jesus). I walked Mike from the pearly gates through a warrior's welcoming parade, which began with Abraham, then Moses, then King David, who walked him before Yeshua.

"I sort of had fun with the Yeshua part as in my mind's eye, seeing the scene as playful with Mike. I sort of nudged Mike along and hinted that the Lord had been pursuing him for quite some time. Of course, I really didn't know how true that was until later, when Roy filled me in. Yeshua then brought Mike before the Father who had some words with him that I don't remember anymore."

Later in the weekend, on Sunday morning, Mike shared that he knew he could no longer deny what he had seen and heard. But, still, he told Rob, "I can't accept your Jesus!"

"Why not?"

He said, "Because I'm Jewish."

Rob told me he gently shook his head back and forth. "What does that have to do with anything? I'm Polish. Big deal. No one is asking you to give up your nationality or heritage. In fact, all I'm trying to do is introduce one Jew to another Jew." Apparently, that shut him up.

Rob continued, "Then, at the end of the day, it played out as you described. I just wanted to pray a blessing over him. But Mike pulled at my arm, got quiet, almost like a child and said, 'I think I want to accept Him, so uhhh... (very New York) whaduido?'"

Rob said, "Just ask Him." Then Mike asked if I would help him along.

"OK, I'll pray and you can pray after me, but it's not about my words. It's about what's in your heart compelling you to want to pray this prayer."

Mike said he understood. The two of them prayed. Mike repeating the critical phrases after Rob. "When we finished praying and I let go of Mike's hand, his eyes got real big and he said, "Whaoooooh! Sum-in just went right tru me. From my head to toes. I'm like tinglin' all over here.'"

"It was all I could do to not bust out laughing. I said, "Well brother, the Scriptures say that when you receive Yeshua as your Savior, the Holy Spirit comes into you.'"

"Mike gave me a quizzical look and said, "Really?'"

"'Yep. Welcome to the family bro.'""

Rob said Mike gave him a big ol' bear hug, and then told him, "You are a warrior!" I just smiled. Others standing nearby, many of whom had prayed for Mike all week, also began hugging him."

Upon hearing the joyous outcome of many months of praying for this man and sharing aspects of my own faith journey with him, I, too, began to tear up. I hugged Rob and thanked him for leading Mike across the finish line.

At the end of the weekend, many of the team members celebrated Mike's salvation at dinner. Roy went out and bought "It's a boy!" balloons for Mike to celebrate his new birthday.

Rob bought a Bible, had Mike's name etched into the cover and sent it to him.

For three days, I cried the entire way driving to work, so thankful to God for Mike's trust in Him. I felt a rush of joy and peace because now, one day down the road, I will see Mike in Heaven. Plus he has Jesus with him here on earth! Praise the Lord!

What an incredible blessing to see a stubborn Jewish guy from

New York City believe in Jesus as his Savior and give his life to Christ! All the time and energy I had put into praying for him and sharing with him felt well worth it. But who am I to take the credit? Some people plant the seeds, some water them, and some reap. God is the one changing hearts and minds. He changed me in a lot of ways through this experience. He reminded me that each of us need others. God had used Roy, Clyde, Rob, and so many other people in Mike's life over the years to tell him about Jesus and to show him what it meant to be a follower of Christ. This was a true example of the body of Christ working together.

From the time I met Mike to the time he trusted in Jesus about two years had elapsed. Some people wait decades to see relatives or friends come to Jesus. And some will never believe; they will die in their sins as the Bible states, but we can't choose for them.

I received lessons of persistence in evangelism, meeting people where they're at, and loving them despite our differences. And I learned to never give up on prayer and God, no matter what happens.

Note

Mike is now at home with the Lord. He died six years after trusting in Jesus. During those six years, Mike faithfully attended a Messianic Synagogue and a Christian church on the weekends. He blessed many through his volunteer work and helping numerous people.

From what Rob understands, Mike became a powerful witness for Christ in his remaining years.

CHAPTER 14

Jehovah's Witnesses— Differences That Matter

MY FIRST ENCOUNTER WITH A Jehovah's Witness came a few years before I talked openly about Jesus or knew much about the differences between Christianity and other religions. I just knew I believed Jesus died, rose again, and would refine my character for the rest of my life. I had asked for forgiveness from my sins and didn't want to ever go back to my old lifestyle.

It was widely known that a unit secretary at the hospital I worked for in Buffalo was a Jehovah's Witness. When I saw her working at the floor desk late one afternoon, I leaned over and asked, "Charlotte, you're a Jehovah's Witness right?"

"Yes," she answered, intently looking at me. "I am."

"Is that Christian?"

"Oh yes," she said.

She turned and continued to answer the multiple ringing phones. Though she told me Jehovah's Witnesses consider themselves Christians, something did not sit right with her answer. I knew the organization differed vastly from fundamental Christianity, but I didn't know how.

Some years later while working at a nursing home in Texas,

I reviewed the medical history for a physical therapy client I planned to see. Just before I closed the chart, I glanced down and saw on the patient's admission's sheet, "Religion—Jehovah's Witness." It's funny how we notice certain things.

I walked into the room of a woman in her late eighties sitting in a wheelchair. She turned around to look at me with her bright white, immaculately styled hair. Another woman—plump, dark-haired, about sixty years old—stood nearby.

"Hi Mrs. Jones, I'm here to work with you on transfers—getting in and out of your wheelchair more easily." I saw a book lying on her bed, a *New World Translation* (NWT)—the book Jehovah's Witnesses use in addition to the King James Version of the Bible. I knew from previous training that the NWT has altered the original Hebrew and Greek so much that it does not correlate with the Bible.

I went through training Mrs. Jones in transferring in and out of her wheelchair several times. Very hard of hearing, she could not answer many of my questions, so her friend Sally filled me in. They knew each other from their Kingdom Hall—a place that Jehovah's Witnesses attend for services.

"How long have you been working here, Pam? I've never seen you before," Sally asked.

"I work for a physical therapy company that contracts with different facilities, so I go where they need me. I'm only here for a week." I also mentioned that I moved from Buffalo to Dallas the previous year to study at Dallas Theological Seminary.

"Really?" Sally said. "I study the Bible all the time. Mrs. Jones and I are both Jehovah's Witnesses, you know. Why don't we get together sometime, and we can discuss things?"

"I could stop back in about half an hour, after I'm finished with work. Will you still be here?"

"I'll wait for you."

"Lord," I prayed as I left the room, "please give me the words to speak, because I don't know too much about their religion, but I know it's different from what I believe about you."

After I signed out for the day, I walked into Mrs. Jones' room again. My heart pounded. I could feel sweat on my body as my face heated up. I didn't know how I could talk to Jehovah's Witnesses about the differences in our faiths.

Sally shared a little about their beliefs. As the conversation turned to who Jesus is, she said, "As a Jehovah's Witness, we believe Jesus was a created being—Michael the Archangel. We believe only in Jehovah. Jesus was a great teacher, but he was not God."

"But Jesus is God," I said. "And He's always been God. I don't know where it's found in the Bible, but Jesus said, 'I and the Father are One.' How could He say that if He weren't God?"

"Oh, honey, you're mixed up. Jesus meant he was given the power through Jehovah to do miracles, but he wasn't God."

"Jesus claimed to be God, and He proved it many times, including through His bodily resurrection," I said.

Sally continued to express her views, including that the body of Jesus dissolved into gases and that he's still Michael the Archangel.

I could feel my ears heating up. "Can I see your King James Bible?" I fumbled through it, looking for some verse or story that I could talk about. "There's no way Jesus was Michael the Archangel. But I don't know where to find what I know about it. I'll have to get back to you."

"Why don't we get together for coffee at my house sometime?" Sally suggested.

"Ah, sure—give me a call." Even thought I had never done anything like that before, I felt God nudging me to be bold in talking with Sally.

After trying to defend my beliefs for an hour, a weight lifted off my shoulders when I left Mrs. Jones' room. Sally seemed to have an answer for everything, while I stumbled around not knowing where to locate things in the Bible. But I felt extremely bad for those two women. After all, I knew they studied the Bible, but they were not worshiping Jesus and having a personal relationship with Him as God. I'd try to prepare myself better for our next meeting.

A few days later, Sally called and gave me directions to her house. For the next week, I researched on Jehovah's Witnesses and what they believe compared to fundamental Christianity. I found major differences. Jehovah's Witnesses think that a limited number of Witnesses can earn the right to go to Heaven—144,000. They have no assurance of eternal life. Jesus, however, never placed a limit for entrance into the Kingdom of Heaven. He repeatedly voiced that He doesn't want anyone to perish and anyone who calls on the name of the Lord shall be saved (Romans 10:13). It is our faith in Christ and repentance through Jesus that saves us—not our performance.

During the drive to Sally's house, I felt nervous again. My personality had some argumentative tendencies in it. Would I be able to articulate what I wanted to say in a loving way? Still not knowing the Scripture verses that well, would I sound ridiculous? I still thought God could use me. I had typed up a handout that cited Biblical references and showed how the founder of the Jehovah Witnesses—Charles Taze Russell—made numerous predictions that never came true. It caused a lot of people pain through the loss of their homes and finances. In addition, because Jehovah's Witnesses do not allow blood transfusions, thousands of people, including children, have died. This is due to their misinterpretation of not eating blood in meat sacrificed to idols. Receiving a blood transfusion to improve someone's health has nothing to do with idolatry.

I wanted so badly for Sally and Mrs. Jones to go to Heaven when they someday died. I longed for them to know who Jesus is—our Savior and God. Sally mentioned that she and Mrs. Jones studied a lot, but they continued to receive false doctrine, apostasy at Kingdom Hall. To simplify, if a person is dogmatically taught for years that one plus one equals three, and someone else comes to show them the truth, that their belief is not correct, it probably is difficult for that person to change their belief. When a person studies under wrong teaching, that's what fills their heart and head.

As I pulled up to her house, I prayed, "Help me, God, to do my best. I trust that the Holy Spirit is in me and will help me. I'm not going to be intimidated by what I don't know."

When I reached Sally's condo, she smiled, invited me in and gave me a cup of hot-brewed tea. She seemed like a pleasant person. We sat in her floral-decorated living room. After some talk about her children and recent retirement from her postal job, I asked her, "How did you choose to become a Jehovah's Witness?"

"I was going through a difficult time. My husband had left me, and I had two small children. I felt lonely and depressed. One day a Jehovah's Witness knocked on my door and asked if they could have a Bible study with me. I agreed. The woman continued to visit every week for studies."

"Did you ever go to a church before she started coming over?"

"I went to a Methodist church off and on. I visited the pastor to ask him what he thought about the teachings of the Jehovah's Witnesses. He couldn't explain things to me like that woman who came to my door did, so I continued the Bible studies. No one ever bothered to call me from my old church, and I never went back. I made new friends at Kingdom Hall."

"Is that pastor you mentioned the only one you asked for help before delving further into the Jehovah's Witness religion?"

"Yes, but as I said, the woman who came to my door, Dolores, was so personable and seemed to know all the answers. She came at just the right time in my life, and I found her Bible studies interesting."

"I'm sorry, Sally, about your husband leaving you. It's too bad that your pastor didn't answer your questions well or direct you to someone who could. How long have you been a Jehovah's Witness?"

"About twenty-five years."

"Sally, I looked up Michael the Archangel." Looking at my notes, I said, "Michael is only listed a few times in the Bible and each time, on his own, could not rebuke Satan (Jude 1:9), yet in Mark 9:25, Jesus rebukes Satan, who was never worshiped while Jesus was." We talked for nearly two hours. Unfortunately, the conversation jumped a lot from topic to topic.

When I left her condo, I felt overwhelmed. As I reflected on the evening during the drive back to my apartment, I knew that I needed to continue to focus more on the important facts. I needed to clearly explain who Jesus is—God from time eternal—and that He does grant eternal life to all who trust in Him through what He did, not what we do. Then, and only then, we have the assurance that we will reside with Him in Heaven for all eternity.

Sally and I met one more time at a restaurant, along with another Jehovah's Witness friend of hers from her Kingdom Hall. I brought my sweet friend Sarah, a fellow student at Dallas Theological Seminary, with me. The conversation again seemed to touch on a lot of our different beliefs, though Sarah and I tried to stick to major points of who Jesus is and that one must be born again to enter the Kingdom of Heaven (John 3:3).

We had a few more months of continued phone conversations, and I invited Sally to my church, but she declined. I continue to pray for her, Mrs. Jones, and their fellow Kingdom Hall congregants to trust in Jesus as their God and Savior and to get out of the apostasy they're in.

God taught me, through these times, that though I have a huge heart for lost souls, He does the saving, not Pam (John 6:44). I can't do everything. I'm one person, but I can try to love and share Jesus with as many people as He shows me to. One day, I will find out the results of these encounters with people of different faiths. I pray that I did make a difference because, just like the lost sheep in Luke 13, every soul matters to Him.

CHAPTER 15

Rich and Poor

"HE'S NOT...?"

"Yes, he is," they told me. "Wait until you see his residence; it's like an art museum."

While living in Dallas, twice a week I visited the apartment of Mr. George, a well-known millionaire, to give him physical therapy. He had undergone back surgery about two months before and was still experiencing quite a bit of pain. The doctor ordered the therapy to improve his flexibility and strength and reduce his pain.

"Hi Mr. George. How's it going today?"

"I'm doing well, thank you. Those exercises you gave me are helping; at least I'm sleeping through the night."

"That's great. With Christmas coming up, I'm sure you'll need that extra energy."

"I don't celebrate Christmas."

"Oh, really. How come?"

"I'm Jewish, and I don't believe in Jesus."

"Oh, I see. Well, I'm sure the exercises will help you during Hanukkah then."

"Yeah, I guess so."

We continued to work together and, one afternoon, I decided out of love to boldly bring him a list of the prophecies from the Old Testament that were fulfilled in the New Testament. There were at least ten signs of the authenticity of Jesus as the Messiah on my sheet of paper, even though I could have written many more.

After we finished therapy, I broached the topic. "Mr. George, I've written out a few things from the Torah—because I wanted to show you how these prophecies came true in the New Testament—when Jesus lived here on earth. They prove how Jesus is the Messiah that the Jewish people have waited and searched for since the beginning of time. I thought you might want to look at them."

Mr. George tilted his head slightly and turned his head to look from his couch. "Listen, it doesn't matter to me."

"I care about you, Mr. George, and I don't understand. Do you ever think about where you'll spend eternity?"

"I'll just be dead, that's it. All I care about is right now." He raised his arm and pointed to the impressive artwork he had amassed and his extravagantly decorated apartment.

"But...Mr. George."

"I don't want to hear it," he said firmly. "I think you need to leave now."

I saw Mr. George one more time for therapy, as physically he was doing well.

About four months after my time ended with Mr. George, I came home in the middle of the afternoon and found my front door slightly ajar. I peeked in and saw an empty entertainment center—a huge blank spot where my television had once sat. I'd been burglarized! In a matter of seconds, my mind sprung into action and my body followed, reluctantly. Because I didn't know whether the perpetrators were still in my apartment, I knew I needed to get out. I ran down the stairs crying, and called 9-1-1.

Shaking and crying, I waited in the parking lot for the police. As the maintenance man walked by, he noticed how upset I was. He went into my apartment to search it for me. "No one's in there now," he said.

The police arrived and carefully went through the apartment and my remaining possessions. They dusted for fingerprints and took a report from me to determine what was missing. The thieves had taken more than $5,000 in jewelry, my TV—and other valuables.

After that day, I continued on with school and work as usual, but I seemed more upset and unsettled than ever. Over the next few weeks, I felt distress setting in. After all, I had moved 1,400 miles to attend Dallas Theological Seminary—so much wanting to please God. I had given up my apartment in Buffalo, quit a stable job of almost nine years, gotten in multiple arguments over the move with my immediate family who ceased talking to me for months, and now I'd been burglarized.

On top of it all I didn't feel well—emotionally, mentally, or physically. "God," I cried, "Why are You letting all these things happen to me when all I want to do is serve You?"

My thoughts quickly went to a previous patient, Mr. George. He appeared to have everything he wanted—money, status, a family—but he remained spiritually poor. I could lose everything—health, family, money, friends, yet my riches far exceeded Mr. George's—I still had Jesus, the only One I really need. Jesus is the sustainer of my life, my reason for being who I am. Jesus is my rock, and I needed to put Him first—not my seminary degree, family, or goals in life, but Him. From that point on, I appreciated the now.

The Bible is clear that everyone goes through times of trouble, but, when Jesus is our center, He can make even the dull days brighter.

They never caught the criminals, but I pray for them, knowing whatever their reasons for robbing me—drugs, greed, that someday they would trust in Christ. I also pray for Mr. George. People need Jesus as their Savior more than anything this earth can offer.

CHAPTER 16

My Patient Greg

THE MAN LAY ON HIS bed with the outline of his ribs showing through his brown colored T-shirt. At forty-five, his wrinkled features and tan skin made him look weathered.

"Hi Greg, I'm Pam. I'm here to do your physical therapy evaluation."

"I've been waiting for this." His voice had a slight edge to it. "I got here several days ago, and no therapy yet."

"I'm sorry. We just don't have enough help."

As I sat on the edge of his bed in the nursing home, I looked at his medical chart—HIV positive, AIDS, lung lesion. Judging by his sagging skin, Greg had lost a lot of weight.

I proceeded to check his joint range of motion and muscle strength, asking him questions along the way.

"So are you from this area?" I asked.

"Yes, been here my whole life. But when I get out of here, I'm going to stay with my family in Oklahoma. Where are you from?" he asked. "You have an accent."

"I moved to Dallas from Buffalo, New York about two years ago to attend seminary—to study the Bible. I work here as a physical therapist only a few days a week. They are very flexible with scheduling my hours."

"Study the Bible? Hmmm, I'd like one of those."

"Oh yeah? What are your beliefs Greg? Do you go to a church?"

"I believe in a higher power. I'm a homosexual, and since I've gotten AIDS, I think a lot more about it. I've tried going to some churches but they want me to change because I'm a homosexual. So now I go to a gay church."

"What do you mean by a higher power? Who is Jesus Christ to you?" I knew we wouldn't have much of a conversation without first laying the groundwork on how he felt about Jesus.

"I believe He lived," he said.

"Have you trusted in Christ, Greg?"

"Not really." He gave me a tentative look.

"You know," I told him, "growing up, I attended church with my family. In my twenties though, I rarely went. I believed in God and Jesus, but did not follow Him. I drank nearly every night of the week, led an immoral lifestyle—not as a homosexual, but heterosexual immorality, and swore a lot. Never did I think about what God or anyone else thought of my actions."

Greg sat on his bed cross-legged, nodding as though he understood. "So what happened after that?"

"In my early thirties, I reached a turning point. I went through some hard times and really wanted to know what love was since often times relationships didn't work out. As a child, I remembered receiving a Bible that had "'God is Love'" on the cover. If God is love, I reasoned, I'm going to open up that Bible and see if it can tell me what real love is."

"I sat down one summer on my carpeted hallway steps and read my Bible. Not just one or two verses, as I had done in the past, but with an intensity—as though I needed help. I started searching for a church in the area. As an analytical person, I went through the list of churches in the yellow pages checking them off as I attended each one. Nothing appealed to me, until a friend suggested a born-again church right down the street from where I lived. "Have you ever heard that term before?"

"Sure," Greg leaned forward, listening intently.

"I found out later that the words 'born again' refer to a person who has trusted in Christ as their Savior. The term is found throughout the Bible."

"During those few months, the Lord worked on me, and years ago, I walked down the church aisle during an altar call and professed my trust in Jesus. Since then, my life has turned completely around in so many ways. I didn't want to get drunk anymore. Some of the growth caused me pain, as I lost some friends who didn't understand the changes in my lifestyle. I'm sure you can see how wanting to please Jesus might cause some friction."

"Yeah, I can see that," Greg still seemed extremely interested in my story.

"I stopped living an immoral life-style, too. Doing that certainly wasn't easy. But overall I felt so much better because I knew I was leading a purer life, a better life than the one before. Now, I need to be clear. None of this happened overnight, and God is still working on me. Believe me, I'm not an easy character."

I looked straight into Greg's eyes. "We can die at anytime— myself included. If you were to die tonight Greg, do you know where you'd go?"

He shook his head while looking down. "No, not really."

"Can I show you something?"

"Sure."

I took out a blank piece of paper from my physical therapy

binder and drew a diagram of God, us, sin that separates, and a cross—the bridge between God and man.

"How do you think a person gets into Heaven?"

"I try to keep the Ten Commandments, and do other good things."

"Greg, do you see on this paper how sin separates us from God? We'll never *do* enough good things to get into Heaven through our own efforts—otherwise why did Christ have to die? It's through trusting in what Jesus *did*, on the cross. The only way to Heaven is through faith in Jesus Christ who forgives you for your sins. He's real love."

"All of those things that changed in my life happened after I trusted in Christ. He's changed me on the inside. Do you understand what I'm talking about?"

"Yes," Greg said, "it's all about trusting in Him. I would like to change myself, too."

"Would you like to trust in Him now?"

"Definitely."

I felt a warmth settle over me, as a comforting thought came to mind: God is so faithful. "Can I pray with you Greg?"

"Sure."

I prayed for Greg to repent and trust in Jesus as his Lord and Savior asking for forgiveness, and he repeated the prayer. Tears welled up in my eyes. I looked up at Greg when I heard him burst out crying. Together, we prayed for Greg's health and for the Lord to give him a peace.

Afterwards he asked, "Can you get me a Bible that I can take home with me when I leave here?"

"Of course." I offered him a small paperback copy of the book of John, which I also had in my binder. He gladly accepted it.

"I work again on Friday, so I'll bring you a Bible then. But I need you to do something really important. Remember this day,

Greg. Especially whenever you doubt, remember that you trusted in Christ. It's a commitment."

"Will you write today's date in the book you gave me?"

After writing it, we talked more about the church he attended that advocated homosexual relationships. "Greg, if I went to a church where the minister said, 'Go ahead, sleep with your boyfriend, it's no big deal. God won't care.' You'd know that's bad theology because God does care."

Since he seemed to be listening intently, I continued. "God made you a man. Without getting into a lot of detail about whatever happened in your life, you were made for a sexual relationship with a woman in marriage or no one, but not another man."

"The church you've gone to that supports homosexual relationships is not teaching the Bible accurately. Instead, it's promoting false doctrine. Greg, I encourage you to find a good, Bible-believing church that can help you to grow in truth and love."

As I got ready to leave his room, I pulled something else out of my therapy binder. I'd recently had an article published in my seminary newspaper, and I just happened to have the paper with me. The newspaper included an article about a former homosexual woman who turned from her sinful lifestyle with support from godly leaders and years later enrolled in the seminary. "Will you read this article please?" I handed it to Greg.

"Thanks, I will."

Interspersed throughout our conversation I had completed my physical therapy evaluation. I gave Greg some exercises to do on his own until therapy again.

"It was great meeting you Pam," he said.

"You too."

I left Greg's room, subtracting the hour I spent talking with him about Christ and praying as personal time off the clock. I knew I'd have to stay late that evening to make up for it, but it didn't matter to me.

Smiling, I silently thanked God for allowing me to show love to Greg in both a tangible and intangible way. With joy in my heart, I headed to the next patient's room.

The Bridge Illustration

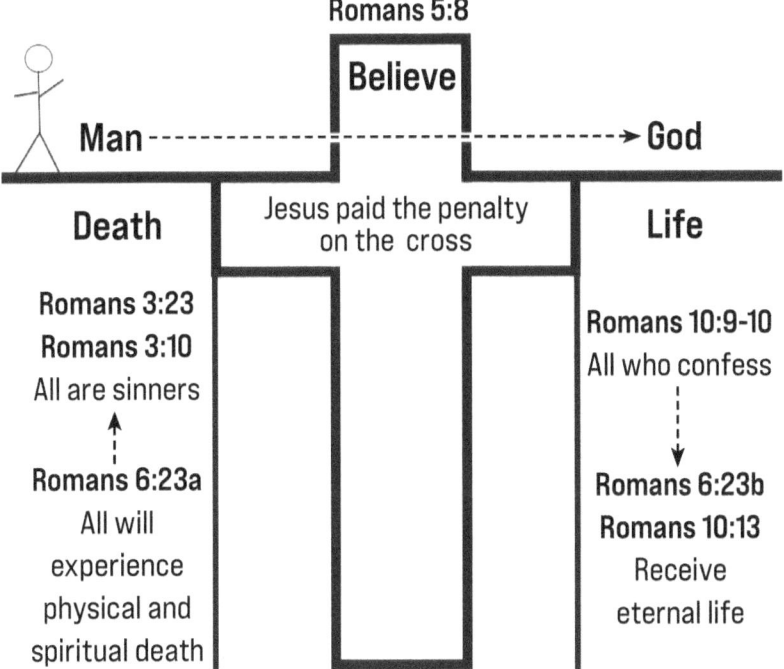

CHAPTER 17

Open My Mouth Wisely

"I PRAYED, AND GOD TOLD me to divorce my husband." A woman I met at a party told me this when I asked about anything new in her life.

"Are you sure about that?" I asked.

"Oh, yes." She nodded her head solemnly before moving on to another topic.

Her statement didn't make sense to me for several reasons, but primarily because she told me that her husband had a mood disorder—he experienced depression at times and she didn't know how to handle it. I wanted to share my thoughts on the matter, but fear overtook me, and—I didn't respond. I didn't know how she and others at the party might perceive my intrusion, but her reason did not sound scriptural at all. The Bible offers only minimal grounds for divorce. Divorce often happens when people react to problems with a hardened heart.

I struggled with what to say to her. Ultimately, I kept quiet—a decision that still haunts me sometimes. You never know how God is going to use people. Had I stepped out in faith to express my view as different from hers based on what the Bible says about divorce, she may have changed her mind. I put my comfort, of not saying anything at the time, above love for her.

Fast forward about two years, after the woman at the party had gotten a divorce and, by that time, married someone else. I always felt guilty that I didn't say more, but their marriage had ended. She had remarried, so I couldn't go back.

Then something similar happened a few years later while living in Dallas. I was working as a physical therapist for a company that provided contract therapy help, and I floated to many different locations. I had only been to this particular nursing home twice before. During lunch with my co-workers, I overhead a very troublesome conversation about a physical therapist, Liz, a petite blonde who complained that she and her husband didn't get along anymore. She felt she had fallen out of love with him.

Another therapist sitting at the table, Bob, spoke in a matter-of-fact tone, "Just get a divorce. You don't want to go through life unhappy anymore, do you? Who would want that?"

Liz nodded her head. Clearly, she readily agreed with Bob.

I couldn't take it anymore. I immediately reflected back to the family party when I had fallen silent about someone seriously contemplating divorce.

When they got up from the table to leave, I approached Liz. "May I talk to you a minute?"

"Sure."

I took her aside in the hall. "I know I don't know you well—in fact, I just met you—but I couldn't help hearing that conversation about your marriage. May I ask you, do you have any faith in God?"

"Yes, I'm a Christian."

I took a deep breath and prayed for wisdom and strength. "Well, you know then that God wants the best for you—always. Bob doesn't know the whole situation, and neither do I. But I can tell you God hates divorce. He wants couples to stay together because, not only did you make a commitment under God, but also getting a divorce will change your whole life and your children's future."

She winced, closed her eyes, and sighed. "It's just so hard though. We've gone for counseling, and it seems like nothing's working."

"Life is hard. So are choices to stay married. I can't imagine what you are going through, but why don't you give it some time? Look at the positives in your husband, not just the negatives. Being incompatible is not a biblical reason to divorce someone."

"I'll think about it," Liz said.

Because I wasn't assigned to that nursing home again, I didn't see Liz at work anymore. I floated to other therapy centers in the Dallas area. One year later, I visited a friend's church in Frisco, Texas, about an hour away from where I lived in Dallas. Charles Swindoll is the pastor of the well-known Stonebriar Community Church. There were at least 3,000 people in the congregation that day.

As I exited through the lobby, I saw Liz. She and a man walked with their arms interlocked.

Our eyes met, and she approached me. "Hi Pam, how are you?"

"Good thanks, and you?"

"Great, I want to introduce you to my husband, Mark. Remember we talked last year? Well, Mark and I are doing very well. We are almost finished building our new house."

"That's really awesome. I'm happy for you."

The conversation, though short, made an impact on me. Open my mouth, and speak God's truth. I don't have control of the outcome, but I control whether I respond in obedience. So far, things had worked out well for Liz and her husband. I learned the importance of sharing who I am and what I know about God's character from the Bible—the guidebook He gave us for living. If we believe it really is an instruction manual for life, we'll trust it and act boldly. You never know what He can do in a situation, where faith is expressed through one follower of Jesus to another person.

Another time, a friend, Jill, and I left the gym together and decided to finish the conversation we'd been having in my car. As we sat talking, she said, "You know Pam, Ryan asked me out for coffee."

"Ryan, the guy who's muscular and bald who walked into the Bible study the other night, late?"

"Yes *that* Ryan. He said he'd like to call me. I didn't give him an answer, yet." Jill said.

"I thought he was married to Christine."

"Well, he was, but they had a lot of problems and got separated about six months ago. Ryan thinks they will probably divorce soon. They've tried counseling and many other things, but nothing has helped."

"Jill, please don't go out with him!" The exasperation I felt burst forth. "He's a married man. Even if it's just for coffee, I'm sure you're both attracted to each other, even on a friend level. You'll only confuse the situation by having a third person involved. Let him work on the marriage without you getting into it."

"You know there aren't many Christian guys in this area— especially good-looking ones. I finally meet someone who has a good job and is interested in me. Aren't I ever supposed to have fun, have a man in my life?"

"Not with him. No, if you leave him alone, the chances are better that they may get back together. When another person gets involved, it takes the focus off healing the marriage and onto the next relationship."

"Jill, I've had this happen in my past. A guy asked me out

years ago. He didn't tell me until a few dates later that he was married but separated."

"When he confessed this to me, I felt shocked and appalled. Before I accepted a date with him, I had specifically asked him if he had ever been married. He told me no—a flat-out lie. When I found out the truth, he told me they planned to divorce within a few months; they hadn't gone through with it yet due to financial reasons."

"I felt confused and messed up. I liked him, but he showed bad character qualities. Even though I wasn't a Christian at that time, I knew inwardly that going out with him again was wrong. My sister strongly advised me to stay far away from him, not only because he was separated, but also because he lied about something so important."

"Initially, I ignored her advice and went out with him one more time, which I painfully regretted. My conscience felt on fire the entire evening. After that, I refused to go out with him again. I even told him I hoped he and his wife got back together. A year later, I ran into him and his wife at a concert in a park, and she was pregnant."

"Starting a new relationship with someone is hard enough, but being the third person makes it very difficult for that person to focus on healing their marriage. It creates emotional entanglements. Ryan and his wife claim to be Christ-followers. They need to choose to get help and fight for their relationship. They made a covenant before God."

She sighed heavily and looked away. "So you're saying I should say no?"

"Yes, seriously, Jill, if you go out with him, I would have a hard time being friends with you."

"What? Why? That's awfully harsh." She crossed her arms.

"Because it's just not right, I mean righteous. It would make me feel like you wouldn't be a very good friend to me, either, if you were ever put in a compromising spot. I'm not trying to be mean. I'm saying this because a friend helps a friend. If you want to look out for Ryan's best interests—and that's what you need to do—put your desires for a man off and pray that he and his wife can reconcile their relationship."

"I see what you are saying; I understand, even though I may not like it." She nodded slightly. "I think you are right about this."

We held hands and I prayed for Jill before she left. "Lord, please keep Jill's relationship with You strong. Guard her heart. Help her to look to you for satisfaction in life and during times of loneliness. If she needs a friend or accountability partner in this situation, help me to encourage her. We pray that you help Ryan and Christine to heal their marriage."

Jill squeezed my hands before she let go.

"You need to stay away from Ryan and let the Lord do the work."

Jill stayed true to her word and turned Ryan down about going out together or talking on the phone to get to know each other more.

About a month later, I saw Ryan with his wife Christine, sitting next to each other in church. That's a good sign, I thought.

In each of these situations, I needed to accept responsibility and act according to God's truth and His prompting. Fortunately, the outcome wasn't for me to determine. And sometimes, as I did on a few occasions, we may look back with regret on what we did or didn't say. However, God is sovereign, and we can trust Him with the situation and the outcome, even if we mess up, which we all do at times.

Often, we don't see the end result of our conversations or prayers until sometime in the future—or until eternity. But as we rely on Him, God is working His plan through our circumstances.

The Bible is always the source of our truth. "Trust in the LORD with all your heart and lean not on your own understanding; in all your ways submit to Him, and He will make your paths straight" (Proverbs 3:5-6).

I like to talk, but my words may not always benefit the listener. It's when we wisely listen first and then speak that we can offer good, godly advice. Fear of intimidation by others can stop many great things from happening. We are not to fear man, but trust and fear God.

CHAPTER 18

Africa—Bound and Determined?

"NO THANKS, I'M NOT INTERESTED." Despite encouragement from fellow classmates at Dallas Theological Seminary to go on a mission trip, I had no inclination. Most of them had gone on and enjoyed multiple mission trips all over the world. But the thought of missions didn't interest me. "I already do enough evangelism and work for the Lord in the U.S. There's no need for me to go out of the country."

Until, of course, God has a way of changing your heart when He desires to. One morning while reading my Bible, I felt God placed a new idea on my heart, "short-term missions." So caught up in the work of going to seminary—most of my recent Bible reading revolved around getting lots of term papers done. My life felt like constant doing, doing, doing and not really "being" with God. I lacked intimate fellowship with Him. I longed to simply spend time sitting at His feet, still and listening for Him. Instead, I tried to conquer the world in ministering to everyone I met, something even Jesus didn't do during His time on earth.

My first reaction to the thought of short-term missions? God isn't prompting me to do this, or is He? I never had a desire to even think about going on a mission trip. I headed to campus that day wondering about this strange idea. I went into the student lounge and proceeded to check the contents of my small locker.

That morning, one announcement in particular caught my eye—a trip to Africa in May. Wow, since childhood, I've always wanted to go to on a safari in Africa. My face lit up. I used to watch episodes of Wild Kingdom and dream about one day exploring those same lands. Of course, I would never seriously book a trip there; it seemed too outlandish.

My heart pounded. This is huge! I thought maybe God was talking to me about a desire I didn't even know I had. I felt nervous, and my heartbeat picked up speed. Had God put that desire on my heart this morning? Could I really go?

Ok, I thought, no harm in going to the informational meeting to find out more about this trip.

A few days later I attended the meeting where I listened to students explain about joining with ALARM (African Leadership and Reconciliation Ministries) to go on a two-week teaching trip to cities in the country of Zambia. On the weekend between the two weeklong visits to Kabwe and Luanshya, anyone from the team who wanted to pay the extra price could go on a safari and see Victoria Falls, the largest waterfall in the world.

As I sat in the meeting, feelings of excitement and fear ran through me. The mission trip would take place about four days after my final exams ended. Could I get everything ready in time? What about the money? What about my family in Buffalo—what would they think? They already thought I had gone crazy for going halfway around the county to attend seminary. Do I even care what my family thinks? If this is stepping out in faith—it could be awesome!

I also knew that it's God's will to spread the Gospel to the world. He tells us clearly to, "Go therefore and make disciples of all the nations, baptizing them in the name of the Father and the

Son and the Holy Spirit" (Matthew 28:19). I wanted to make a difference for Him.

Nervous but excited, I sent out support letters for finances and prayer, got my required shots, and, of course, told my family in New York of the trip. Again, they thought, I'd flipped. I knew I wanted to obey God, and I believed in my heart that, even as a child, I'd had a strong desire to go to Africa. I wanted to step out in faith and do this.

After classes and finals ended for the spring semester, I had only a few short weeks to prepare my teaching material. The two-week trip focused on teaching pastors and teachers, so they could carry that forward to their churches. Fellow classmates from seminary—Yvette, and four men, and I would meet the team members from ALARM in Lusaka, the capital of Zambia, and go on from there. I would be teaching the book of Ruth and a functional topic on establishing a women's ministry in the local church.

The trip, the experience, the entire adventure for Jesus amazed me. I love teaching and even incorporated my physical therapy techniques into some of the classes by exercising during breaks. Never one to sit still for long, I figured the women would enjoy the afternoon stretching and lunges. They did! I also took nightly walks with Beatrice, one of the leaders from ALARM, and that added to my enjoyment of seeing the local areas and spending time with her.

One man at the conference showed up on Thursday of the trip. I spotted him sitting in the gravel, outside of the conference hall. Beatrice told me he had just arrived.

As I greeted him, I had to know. "The conference started Monday. "Why are you so late?" And then I looked down and saw his legs—very thin, shriveled, and hardened callouses covered his knees.

"I've been crawling since Saturday."

The women at the conference, me, and Yvette

The women who
made us lunch and me

Teaching the women with a translator next to me.

Jeff, Mark, the guide, and me while on our safari

Part of a herd of elephants.
So great to see!

"Crawling, what happened to you?"

"I've had polio since I was a child."

"Where's your wheelchair?"

"I've never had one."

I stared at him—in complete shock. The man, who said his name is Franco, had to be in his mid-to-late 30's.

"I heard that people were coming from the U.S. to teach the Bible, and I wanted to be here."

I nearly gasped, but held myself back. Thoughts of compassion flooded me, as I clearly witnessed this man's faith put into action. "Do you need help getting inside?" They had started the teaching session about two hours before.

"No, I can make it," he said.

"Crawling? No, I insist people will carry you in." I ran into the conference center, grabbed some guys, and they lifted him into a seat. We also got him some food to eat.

After he made it inside, I walked to the back of the center. I leaned against a building, and I burst out crying, sobbing. What dedication! I would never see anything like that in the United States. In the hospitals I've worked for, there are wheelchairs up and down the halls and available for nearly everyone who needs one. Not in Zambia. This man, crippled since birth, had never owned one his entire life.

Beatrice hurried to me when she saw me crying. I talked with her about the man. "It's common to see people pulling themselves along the rough terrain on their knees. Healthcare is not good here, but for those who know Jesus, He means everything to us," she explained.

The events of that day left a deep impression on me. I felt weak, sick, and—at the same time—awestruck by Franco crawling so far on his knees, simply because he wanted to know Jesus better.

For lunches, the women worked outside over steel drums

making rice, nshima (made from ground maize and water), and meat. We had other foods, including watermelon and bananas. Flies buzzed around the drums where the women stirred the food. I ate what I could, but ended up losing several pounds.

On the weekend between the two-week trip, four out of the six members in our group went to another location in Livingstone, Zambia, named after David Livingstone, the Scottish missionary. We went on a Safari in Chobe National Park, Botswana. What an ordeal to get there! We had to bargain with people for our transportation in buses and a barge, and ended up about an hour and a half late. I fretted, fearful that we would travel all this way to Africa and be left behind. I hated to possibly miss the safari. Thankfully, Zambians have a more relaxed way of living than time-driven Americans—me included. The people who ran the safari had waited for us to arrive.

In the open top Jeep with our guide, we saw hundreds of animals fairly close to us! Wild boars, crocodiles, elephants, and lions were among the many. Our guide impressed me with his vast knowledge of the terrain and the animals.

We traveled to Victoria Falls where we saw monkeys walking on the street. In fact, the bus had to stop several times to wait for them to get out of the way. The beauty and majesty of Victoria Falls took my breath away! The thunderous falls, which border the countries of Zambia, Zimbabwe, and Botswana were loud and powerful. We also saw a gorgeous rainbow over the three countries.

As we walked along the streets looking for a place to eat dinner, we came across numerous children begging for food and money. A large group of them congregated outside of a certain bakery. When we left the bakery, I had bought some food to give to them, but my heart ached for these kids. At dinner-time, we sat down to eat at the Funky Monkey Restaurant.

I sat there for all of two minutes, until I couldn't stand it any more. No doubt, we were wealthy Americans, by their standards. And it seemed so wrong to order whatever we wanted on the menu and enjoy a delicious meal without a care in the world. I thought of the children begging for a meal just outside the restaurant.

I walked up to the manager. "I want to bring some of these kids in."

"That's fine," he said.

We chose two boys, Junior and David and we invited them to join us for dinner. Mark and Jeff took them to the men's bathroom so they could wash up. I wondered whether they practically needed to take a bath in there, which might get us kicked out of the restaurant before we could even eat.

The boys ate their meals in complete silence, but I found later they both lived on the streets since their parents died from AIDS. "Isn't there somewhere you can go—an orphanage, a church?"

They shook their heads, no.

I asked the waiter to bring them something nutritious to eat and milk to drink—not soda, which initially they started to order. Aged ten and twelve, they both looked about five years younger because of their small stature and thin bodies.

After dinner we left the restaurant and said good-bye to the boys. I told them I would pray for them even when we went back to the United States. I thought I'd never see them again.

But the next day, we were getting ready to leave to meet the rest of the team for the next week of teaching. As Mark, Jeff, and I walked along the path, I saw two children ahead of us on the other side of the road sleeping face down on the sidewalk.

"Wouldn't it be weird if that was Junior and David? Let's go over and see." I started to cross the road.

I called, "Junior? David?" The boys stood up. It was them!

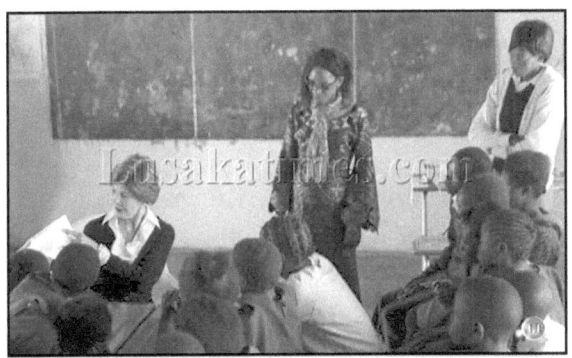

Former First Lady Laura Bush visiting the school with
Mutinta Mwananyanda (standing) and another teacher.
(Used with permission from Lusaka Times)

We talked to them a little while, and I gave them both a few dollars. Looking back, I wish I had bought them new clothes or done more for them. I still pray for Junior and David's safety and provision.

After returning to the States, I realized what a profound effect the mission trip to Africa had on my life. It taught me many lessons. I don't need that much to feel comfortable. So much of America focuses on materialism, while millions of people around the world are starving to death. I determined to learn to live a simpler life. My self-control in spending changed dramatically. God could do so much more with my money—helping others who need to know Him and providing them with resources to stay alive.

The people in Africa need our help. There are needs in the United States and the entire world, but God opened my eyes to the AIDS crisis, homeless children and adults who lacked food, proper clothing and shoes, and a severe lack of quality medical care and education. Yet, through it all, I saw Franco and the people at our teaching conferences rejoicing in the Lord. They sang loudly and boldly worshipped Him in the schools where we taught. Despite cultural distinctions, people who know Jesus have more commonalities than differences.

As our group prepared to leave Zambia, some of the women asked if they could contact Yvette and me via email. One of the women at the conference, Mutinta Mwananyanda, runs a Christian School in Kabwe, Zambia, Salvation and Healing Ministries. Mutinta and I started emailing each other when I got back to the States. To this day, we keep in touch weekly. It's amazing how, even though we are thousands of miles away and live in vastly different countries, we still have much in common because of Jesus. We think similarly. We each ask for prayer for people. We share areas in our lives that we struggle with.

Most of the children in her school get one meal a day. Some are orphans living on the street due to their parent's death at a young age. I'm so glad I can help them, even in a small way, through donations, prayer, and sometimes a word of encouragement to Mutinta. Though I help, they still need many others to want to make a difference.

I ask those reading this today—instead of buying another purse, coffee cup, or trinket that you may never use anyway—how about helping those in need? Whether in this country or overseas, we are the hands and feet of Christ sent to do His will, both in word and deeds. Let us do this now—not ten years later—and leave the results to Him.

If anyone would like to donate to the Zambia, Africa, *Bana Besu Feeding Project* and *Lufutuko Community School*, here is their contact information:
Mutinta Mwananyanda at shministries2003@gmail.com

Facebook: Bana Besu Feeding Project or Lufutuko Community School and Bana Besu Feeding project

CHAPTER 19

The Prayer

DID YOU EVER PRAY TO God about something and expect Him to answer? A lot of people say they pray to Jesus, and hopefully they mean that, but do you expect Him to answer or give you specific directions? He did for me.

After going on my first mission trip to Zambia, Africa, I returned home to Dallas, Texas excited, yet exhausted at the same time. I felt invigorated after teaching the women at our two-week conferences, spending time with the ministry team and missionaries, and witnessing the beauty of the country, the exotic animals on our safari, and Victoria Falls.

My schedule the past several years had been grueling. Yet I had brought much of that on myself. I attended Dallas Theological Seminary full-time, including most of the summers. I also worked as a physical therapist, volunteered in ministry, and did the normal everyday housework and chores that needed to get done. I also tried to keep in touch with people and maintain some friendships. Overall though, I felt quite tired most of the time.

As I rested on my couch one afternoon, I prayed and asked God silently what to do with my degree when I graduated. After moving all the way from New York State to Texas to attend seminary, I really didn't have a specific career path for when I finished school. I really just wanted to know Jesus more through His Word, so that I could communicate His truths better to others.

As I lay on my couch praying, the answer came. Bring wheelchairs to Zambia. What? I thought, was that God? Immediately I thought of Franco, the man I met who crawled for four days to come to one of our conferences in Zambia. I could imagine giving money to help those in Africa, but giving wheelchairs? That would far exceed anything I'd ever thought of doing.

I remembered the verse about testing the spirits in the Bible. I needed to make certain I had heard God talking to me through the Holy Spirit. And so I prayed. God, if that was You, if this is Your will, please confirm it through Scripture.

I opened my Bible. I had chosen to read chapter by chapter through various books, and I recently read 1 Corinthians. "This service that you perform is not only supplying the needs of God's people but is also overflowing in many expressions of thanks to God. Because of the service by which you have proved yourselves, men will praise God for the obedience that accompanies your confession of the Gospel of Christ, and for your generosity in sharing with them and with everyone else" (2 Corinthians 9:12-13).

God confirmed for me through Scripture, exactly what He wanted me to do. He let me know that supplying those in need in Zambia with wheelchairs would glorify Him. I wanted to obey Him, but what about the need? Specifically, how would I connect with people who needed wheelchairs?

A few days after my prayer, I sent an email to Mutinta, a woman who attended one of the week- long conferences. I told her that I would like to help provide wheelchairs to Zambians in need.

About a month later, I got more confirmation of the answer to my prayer. I walked out to my apartment postal box and found inside a large manila envelope. The envelope contained a letter from Pastor George Lewanika of Resurrection Faith Care Ministries in Zambia, along with many pictures of disabled people without legs. He had listed the names of twenty people requesting mobility aids. Here was the specific need.

Now I'm involved, I thought. I need to do something. I started looking everywhere for ministries involved with wheelchairs. I found a couple of organizations I thought had potential, but none of them went to Zambia.

After hitting several closed doors, not finding a wheelchair supplier, I started to feel frustrated. I prayed again. God, if you want me to bring wheelchairs to Zambia, I need You to show me where to find them. I'm hitting dead ends everywhere.

Soon after I prayed, having just completed all my requirements for my degree, I attended my last day of seminary chapel. A professor, Dr. Dorian Coover-Cox, with whom I had lunch one time, ran up to me with an excited look on her face.

"Pam, are you still looking to get involved in a wheelchair ministry?"

"Yes, but I can't find one that goes to Zambia."

"I've been looking for you." She handed me a piece of paper with a phone number on it. "Try calling them," she said. "A family member of mine told me about a wheelchair ministry, or something similar called PET International, based in Florida. My family thinks they help those in poor countries who need wheelchairs."

I contacted the organization and found out they manufacture and ship hand-driven three wheeled cars to third world countries. You need to use your hands to turn a wheel, and there's a small trunk-like part in the back so they can carry things. PET stands for personal energy transportation. I felt absolutely elated when I learned Zambia was one of their destinations! The ministry that gifts the wheelchairs shares the Gospel and makes sure each person truly needs the device. They also teach the recipients how to use and care for the PET before gifting it to them.

Little by little, I secured the money needed for the PETs. This took a few months. Nearly a year after my initial prayer asking Jesus what to do with my degree, the people on the list from Resurrection Faith Ministries got their mobility aides. Delbert and Sandy Groves, missionaries at the New Life Center in Zambia delivered the PETs along with Pastor George Lewanika. They had a ceremony and prayer time also.

Several months later I received another large envelope in the mail. Reverend George sent me pictures of many happy faces of people sitting on their new PETs. People who had previously crawled on their knees to go anywhere, literally looking in the dust, could now move around freely. It felt like such a blessing to help them.

God amazed me in this situation by directly answering my prayer and confirming it overtime through Scripture, circumstances, and godly counsel. It's so neat how sometimes we pray, and He gives us an answer; other times, we need to wait and keep seeking Him for His direction.

I used to think of God as far away up in the sky, not really wanting to help me. Or wondering why would He care about little old me when He's got so many more important things to do. That perception is far from accurate. He cares about each of us (1 Peter 5:7) and the impact we can make on one another for His kingdom. He loves us and wants to prosper us, despite trials we may go through. "For I know the plans I have for you, plans to prosper you and not to harm you, plans for hope and a future" (Jeremiah 29:11). I need to believe the verses that I read, not just memorize them for a test, or say them to sound impressive that I know the Bible.

We can count on God and trust Him as we communicate

Delbert and some of the PETs recipients

with Him through prayer. Just like talking with another human being, He wants us to talk with Him. Communing with God is a two-way street—we need to listen and spend our time wisely in prayer and reading His Word. Spending time with Jesus is the only way to grow closer to the Lord. Jesus is the Word. He's the living God.

I'm thankful God gave me the inspiration and desire to help those who needed wheelchairs. He is so faithful to care for us. Yet there is much more for us to do.

If anyone would like to donate to The PET Project in Zambia, Africa, here is their contact information:

Facebook: PET Zambia

Websites: PetZambia.org, www.NewLifeZambia.org

Any further questions: Delbert & Sandy Groves at groves@newlifezambia.com

CHAPTER 20

Conversation Over Shoes

AS I BROWSED A LOCAL department store one day, I decided to wander over to the shoe aisle. There they sat—cute, bright white, wedge sandals. I'll try them on, I thought. A woman sat on the bench with the attached mirror trying on shoes as well. She had a pile on the floor in front of her.

She glanced my way as I seated myself at the other end of the bench. "Those look cute."

"Thanks, but I don't know." Her comment and my response heightened my internal debate. Maybe it's best I don't buy them—especially since I'm considering a job with a ministry that doesn't pay much. Plus I probably have sixty pairs of shoes already.

A thin man with gray hair and a mildly-slouched posture gave me a look around the corner of his cart. "They look great on you; you should get them," he said.

The friendly woman continued talking away as if she'd known me for much longer than just a few minutes. "I had knee surgery a few months ago. This was the first time I've been able to make it out and get some new shoes."

"Oh really, I'm a physical therapist." I remarked. We talked a little about her knee surgery and some of the exercises she was doing.

"Where do you work?" she asked.

"Nowhere right now. I moved back to the area a few weeks ago. I was in Dallas getting my Master's Degree in Christian Education. I have to decide whether I was to use my degree in Christian education or go back to working as a P.T."

Peggy then formally introduced herself and her husband, John. "My daughter and her husband are in the process of relocating to Dallas," Peggy said. "You indicated that you graduated with a degree in Christian education. My daughter's friend has cancer and has been having a spiritual person praying for her. What do you think of that?"

"I guess it would depend on who they're praying to. Are they Christian, Buddhist, Hindu, something else, or just mixing it all up? I know Christ heals, but if they're praying to a god that doesn't exist, they might as well pray to the air. There's only one God—God the Father, Son, and Holy Spirit. Only the real God hears prayers."

"I'm not sure what they believe," Peggy said, as she continued trying on her multiple pairs of shoes.

"What about you?" I asked. "Have you trusted in Jesus?"

"Yes, I have," she said.

"And your husband?"

"Well, he's Jewish."

Standing by his cart that by now contained about four or five pairs of women's shoes, I turned towards him. Knowing that it took courage to share one's faith with a stranger, I asked God to make me brave. "Are you Jewish?"

"Yes," he replied.

"What kind of Jewish are you: Orthodox, Reformed, Conservative, or Messianic?"

"Reformed."

"I love Jewish people," I said. "Jesus was a Jew. How do you view Jesus?"

"He was a good man, a teacher. He set an example for us."

"Oh, He did a lot more than that. Look at all the miracles He performed, including raising Lazarus from the dead. Have you ever read the New Testament? It fits perfectly with the Torah."

"I never really looked into it. I was instructed as a child, but I haven't read much more since then," he said.

"What do you do with your time?" I asked him.

"I'm a retired banker, but I still consult on the stock market."

"I suggest you sit down and read the Bible, especially the book of Matthew whose recipients were primarily Jewish. Did you know there are over three hundred prophecies recorded in the Torah that came true over 2,000 years later? Jesus claimed to be God and He proved it. He promises everlasting life to those who believe. Since trusting in Him, He has definitely changed my life."

"I'll think about it," John said.

"Both my dad and brother died suddenly, so I encourage you don't wait until it's too late. There are lots of Messianic Jewish congregations in the area. You could check them out. They still have the Jewish customs, but they have embraced Jesus as the Messiah. That's why we don't have to sacrifice animals for our sins anymore. Jesus was the perfect blood sacrifice."

After a little more conversation, I felt I needed to get going. We talked about a restaurant near where my family lived. I handed them a slip of paper, "Here's my phone number, in case you ever want to get together for coffee or dinner." John gave me the name of a book to read on stocks.

I decided not to buy those shoes that day, but I got a lot more enjoyment out of my hour-long store conversation with Peggy and John. I pray that one day John will trust in Jesus as his Savior and that I see them both in Heaven. Maybe Jesus will have a pair of white wedge sandals waiting for me when I get there.

CHAPTER 21

My Roman Catholic Friends

"IF I WANT TO GO, I'll let you know."

"Marissa, you're always complaining you don't have many friends. Here's your chance to meet some. Why don't you come to the party? It's a friendly group, you'll feel comfortable."

"Like I said, Pam, I'll get back to you."

Marissa often seemed down and critical about her life, calling it boring. So being the more extroverted of the two of us, I invited her to many functions and parties. She rarely said yes. Sometimes she would accept an invitation to see a movie or go for a walk in the summertime. She turned me down so many times; I don't know why I kept trying. The only thing I could think of was our lengthy friendship. Despite her ongoing complaints, I longed for her to have a happier life—obviously more than she wanted to change and get rid of some of her fears.

Our long time friendship had spanned more than half of our lives, though we seemed like an unlikely pair. Marissa is reserved, methodical, and structured; she has a wonderful, sweet smile, which she reveals when people open up to her. I, on the other hand, love parties, and manage a busy-but-organized life. I truly enjoy spending time with people.

During Marissa's college years, she went to many social activities—mostly drinking related. After graduation, she took a job at a financial institution. With that change, she turned more inward. She gets up early in the morning to go to work, exercises at the gym three times a week, and stays overnight at her mother's house one evening on the weekend. She also goes to Catholic mass weekly. Although surrounded by people at these events, she rarely initiates conversations to spark a new friendship.

"Pam, I'm not like you. I can't talk to people I just met and feel comfortable."

"Well, that's why you have friends like me—to get you going—and I need a friend like you to calm me down. To make friends, you have to step out of your comfort zone and be friendly. Marissa, I can't force you to make changes in your life. You have to want to."

I often invited her to my Sunday church service or singles' events where people came from many different congregations across the area.

"Pam, I'm Catholic, and I'm never going to change religions, so quit trying."

My reply usually went something like this. "I go to a Christian church. I would love if you would visit sometime with me and hear the pastor preach. You'll love the worship music too. My church uses the Bible a lot, and I think you'd really enjoy the service. Just come once."

After a year of my encouraging her, she agreed to meet me one Sunday morning. I loved the service—the preaching, the music, everything.

"What did you think?" I asked as soon as we exited the sanctuary into the lobby. I smiled, expecting she'd have the same reaction as I did—wonderful.

She turned around while walking ahead of me. "It certainly

was different from where I go. I have to leave now. I have plans." She scurried off to find her car.

A few weeks later, Marissa and I were discussing current issues in each other's lives over the phone.

"Will you pray for me about this?" I asked her.

"Ok, I will." Silence.

"I meant now, on the phone, so I can hear you."

"Pam, if I pray for you, you're probably not going to like the way I do it."

"That's O.K. I'd really appreciate you praying out loud though."

"Mother, Mary of God"….she continued with a rote prayer including listing a saint.

"Marissa, what was that?" I blurted out without thinking.

"I told you, I pray different than you do."

"Marissa, you don't have to pray to anyone but God—Jesus, who's our mediator."

"You don't respect my religion, I'm Catholic."

"I respect you as a person, Marissa, but I don't agree with everything you believe. The Bible teaches us to pray directly to Him. We're to obey Scripture, not our traditions. We must always test to see if teaching lines up with what Jesus shows us."

"Well in my religion, that's how we do it."

"Marissa, the pope or a minister is not above Jesus. They're just people, imperfect. Look for yourself in the Bible. It doesn't say to talk to Mary or a saint—only God. The disciples actually rebuked people who tried to do that. How about if we look in the Bible together sometime, and you can see for yourself?"

"I'm not talking to you about this anymore. I have to go." She hung up the phone without saying good-bye.

Ugh, I thought. I hope I didn't sound argumentative, but I wondered if she ever considered the words she uses. It's dangerous when anyone believes everything a priest or a pastor tells them without validating it for themselves through God's Word.

But Marissa and I had known each other for over twenty years. I felt invested in her life. I try to talk with her and reason with her, but she doesn't want to hear it. I could have kept my mouth closed, but because I care about her, I felt I needed to ask her questions.

Roman Catholicism is prevalent living in New York State. Years ago, while working at Buffalo General Hospital, I overhead a floor nurse say to another hospital worker, "I know I'm going to Heaven because of my necklace."

I stopped reading the chart in my hands and looked over at her. "Sandi, what would make you think that if you wore a particular necklace you'd go to Heaven?"

"My priest told us that."

"Have you ever checked your Bible? We go to Heaven because of faith in Jesus as our Savior, not what we wear or do for Him."

"Well, that's what I learned," she said before she walked away to treat a patient.

I felt frustrated by her response because of what it told me about her attitude and her approach to faith. Do people simply believe what they're told? Don't they question others, even those in authority?

Another incident happened while I attended Dallas Theological Seminary. I received a nice letter from my friend Laurie's mother, Sheila. Laurie told her mom that I moved to Dallas to get a degree in Christian education. Sheila's letter talked a lot about Roman Catholicism. In it, she urged me to accept their belief system.

Sheila and I sent letters back and forth over a six-month period. Our major points of disagreements included praying to saints or Mary, believing in purgatory, elevating Mary to the same level as God, and allowing Catholic church tradition to take precedence over the teachings of the Bible.

I cited several Scripture verses to Sheila:

"All Scripture is God-breathed and is useful for teaching, rebuking, correcting and training in righteous, so that the man of God may be thoroughly equipped for every good work" (2 Timothy 3:16).

"For there is one mediator between God and men, the man Christ Jesus" (1 Timothy 2:5).

"In the same way, the Spirit helps us in our weakness. We do not know what we ought to pray for, but the Spirit Himself intercedes for us with groans that words cannot express. And He who searches our hearts knows the mind of the Spirit, because the Spirit intercedes for the saints in accordance with God's will" (Romans 8:26-27).

After much dialogue via mail, Sheila and I ended communication. Even though I didn't agree with her, I wanted her to understand that it is through faith alone—in who Christ is and what He did on the cross—that we are saved. Our church denomination or our acts of service do not get us into Heaven.

I assured Sheila in one of my letters that I loved Jesus and had trusted in Him with my life and I hope she would, too.

As for Marissa, I continue to pray for her to have a personal relationship with Jesus and to conquer her fears. We need to compare church teachings to Scripture, and, if they don't match up, especially on important beliefs, find a different church or denomination that does teach the Bible accurately.

Thankfully, Marissa and I have remained good friends, despite our differences.

CHAPTER 22

Long-Haired Larry

I MET LONG-HAIRED LARRY IN Williamsville, New York, over twenty years ago. His matted hair trailed all the way to his knees. He completed his look with a scruffy beard and dirty, old clothes. I often saw him turning in garbage bags full of empty cans at a local supermarket. Probably in his late fifties or sixties, he had many lines on his face showing how he'd braved the rugged weather conditions. From what I heard, Larry had lived on the streets near a busy highway for over thirty years.

Occasionally, I'd see Larry sipping his coffee in a booth at McDonald's or at a table in a local coffee shop. He looked lonely. I started making it a habit of saying hello to him. With a small wave and a low voice he'd say hi back.

I felt bad for Larry as I would anyone who is homeless, especially in the Buffalo area with cold temperatures and lots of snow. Who could bear sleeping outside? So far, he had.

I kept thinking about that unusual looking man I'd see sometimes while getting groceries. I finally called a downtown church that helped homeless people.

"What he looks like on the outside is what he feels like on the inside," the man on the phone told me.

"Really," I said. "What can I do? "

"Make friends with him; it's a slow process. You can offer him some socks—show that you care."

Over the next few weeks I saw Larry sitting in the booths—always looking down at his coffee, not up at the customers. No one sat with him or talked to him. Did he not have anyone who cared about him—family, friends, anyone? I thought. I had no idea what had gotten him into his current condition—the Vietnam War, mental issues, addictions, or just his own choices?

Credit: Anne Neville/Buffalo News

Larry

I approached him one day, tray in hand. "Larry, can I sit with you?"

"Sure," He smiled a bit and sat up straighter.

I sat across from him and introduced myself. For the next few minutes it felt like a one-way conversation, me asking questions, commenting on the weather or something trivial.

"Do you work Larry?" I asked.

"I pick up cans."

"Oh, ok, did you ever work for a business?"

"As a cook a long time ago."

"Did you go to school for that?"

"Erie Community College," came his short reply.

"Really, how come you don't do it anymore?"

"I don't know."

"Larry, where do you sleep at night?"

"I got a room on Kensington Avenue," he said.

That's not what I heard, I thought. He doesn't want to admit being homeless.

"Larry, how come you live like this? You know Jesus loves you. He wants the best for you and I know that he wouldn't want you living on the streets or in the woods. Have you ever tried to get help from an agency or homeless shelter?"

"Nah, I'm OK."

My direct approach led to little response.

After that, every few weeks and months, I'd stop by and sit across from him while I ate a sandwich. I offered to get him one, but he declined every time. I'd tell him jokes. I tried to help him, I wanted to help him. I talked to him about Jesus and asked him if he ever prayed to trust in Him.

"Larry, I'd like to sit with you if you'd meet me at the church across the road from here this Christmas Eve?" He nodded in agreement. I drove to the church Christmas Eve and couldn't find Larry anywhere near where we were to meet. I felt very disappointed.

I prayed for Larry and his situation privately. "Lord, what else can I do?"

When near his area of town, sometimes I'd bring friends with me to visit Larry. Maybe cheer him up—show him people do care. Maybe they would have ideas to get him out of the situation that he was in. Nothing changed.

When I decided to move to another state, before I left, I told Larry about it and that I'd be praying for him regularly and wouldn't forget him. "I hope you stay safe, Larry. And, please, you really need to get some medical care, dental too. I'll put you in a taxi now and you can go. Would you?"

"I'll think about it," he answered every time.

On vacations, when I came back to Buffalo—I'd occasionally

stop at the places Larry hung around at, and most of the time, I'd see him—just like I had several years before.

"Larry, do you remember me?"

"Yeah, Pam."

Wow, I felt shocked knowing that he remembered my name.

After finishing seminary, I moved back to Western New York. Larry still showed up at the same places that I saw him before.

A few months ago, I noticed a loss of hair on the right side of his head.

"Larry, you really need to see a doctor. There's obviously something wrong."

"I'm OK," he responded.

A friend recently told me she thought Larry has unmedicated schizophrenia. If that's true, he probably needs some medication. Whatever his issues, without others and supernatural intervention from God, and willpower by Larry, he may never change. I don't know if he has that illness, but I really do love him as a person.

He's someone who has changed my perception on some things including, patience, the fact that we can't control another, and most of all my ability to let go of my worry. I barely knew the man and worried about him.

I started out wanting Larry to change into how I would want to see him—a haircut and basic grooming, a regular job, an apartment, a car, and friends. By and large, Larry didn't change, but I did. I began to accept him for who he was. Maybe I've learned to be less judgmental. Larry's choices aren't what I would have for him, but, just like God has done for each of us, He gives us choices but doesn't force Himself on us.

Though I longed to help Larry, I couldn't fulfill his needs or change his medical condition or current living situation. I could offer him advice, take the initiative in conversations, pray for him, and introduce him to more friends of mine. Yet ultimately, it's still his choice to stay where he is, or change.

Though others may present themselves in a slightly different way, Larry's story is repeated in thousands of instances all over the U.S. Sometimes, they look good on the outside—they wear nice clothes, have a beautiful house to live in, and have good mannerisms—but feel terrible on the inside. Sometimes people hide behind a facade—because they can. People in Hollywood, for instance, seem to have so much, yet you read countless stories of many turning to drugs, alcohol, sex, and suicide. They need help, just as I have at times, when I could see no way to change myself or my circumstances.

Just knowing people casually—completely on a surface level—but not really seeing inside their life, it's easy to get fooled into thinking you're the only one who has problems. The Bible says that in this world you will have trouble (John 16:33). We all go through troubles, some worse than others. Do you realize God is there to help? Ultimately, the Lord is the best comforter. We just need to know Him and seek Him despite—or because of our infirmities.

That's the part that requires trust. I regularly pray for Larry's protection and health, but most of all, I pray for him to follow after Jesus. Maybe one day, he will have a warm place to spend Christmas, with people he loves who love him in return.

Note

Larry was found dead of hypothermia in a bus shelter on a freezing cold, blizzard-like day. He refused help or shelter offered him during the storm. I knew one day Larry would probably die this way, but still the news came as a shock to me and to the community he lived in.

Three days before he died, I drove down the street he usually frequented. I hadn't seen him in about a year, though I had tried looking for him on numerous occasions. I stopped at McDonald's, but he wasn't there.

The morning he died, as I drove to work, I prayed for Larry. I don't know when he died, but he was on my heart.

It's so sad Larry died in the bitter cold. Perhaps he thought he was tough enough to withstand the frigid weather, as he had for many decades living on the streets. Or maybe, he felt sick that day and because he was used to saying no to others, he didn't know how to say yes, to accept, or seek help. Maybe he just sat at the bus shelter thinking the bus would come soon.

We don't know what went through Larry's mind that day or any day. Larry was an independent man. Although we really didn't know him well, many people folks in the neighborhood loved him. I did share the Gospel with him a few times over the years. Since he was a man of few words, I don't know if he truly believed in Jesus as his Savior, but he nodded in agreement. I hope I will see him again one day in Heaven with Jesus and all the other believers.

CHAPTER 23

A Mormon Belief System

"PAM, THE NEIGHBORS ARE HAVING their holiday party. Are you going?" my mom asked.

"Yeah, but I need to do a few things first, so I'll see you there in about an hour."

A little while later, I walked across the street to the brightly lit house. A number of cars lined the sides of the road. Karen and Gary, who held festive parties several times a year, often had many friends over. Their faces beamed when entertaining and sharing their home with others.

Upon entering their house, their chubby, furry dog, Samantha, ran up to meet me. "He's so cute," I said as I petted him and his swaying body. Primarily older relatives of Gary and Karen's stood around their kitchen island munching on various appetizers. I remembered from last year that some members of their family, especially those from further away, were Mormons. Last year when I left a party of theirs, I had prayed for God to use me. "Jesus help me to interact with people that aren't believers including Mormons, to help them to come into an authentic relationship with you."

Perhaps tonight was the night. After filling my plate with

deviled eggs, roast beef, shrimp, and different salads, I sat down at their cherry dining room table. I saw a little girl about three years old with long brown hair and ruby lips that I met the year before. I'd wanted to play with her then, and she ran to her mother crying when I had tried to approach her. A year older now, she seemed a little more receptive when I smiled, and she actually smiled back.

The majority of people, however, I had never met before. A man in his late sixties sat down on the corner of the table next to me and we struck up a conversation.

"My wife Jane and I are from Virginia. We come up every year around this time to visit. My son and his new wife just graduated from Brigham Young. Here's my son now."

"Hi, I'm Cody." A tall man with blonde hair shook my hand and sat down a few seats away with another whopping plate of food.

"Hey Cody. Your father was telling me that you and your wife just graduated from Brigham Young. So what did you take there?"

"Teaching, I'm certified in math education and my wife has a degree in elementary education."

"Have you started looking for a job yet?"

"Yes, I'm subbing temporarily and looking for a job in the Buffalo area. My wife, Amanda, found a full-time teaching job that will start in January."

"Well, I'm sure you'll find something permanent soon."

"So, Pam, your mom tells us that you just moved back from Dallas?" Cody's father seated to my right asked.

"Yes, I did."

"What made you move back?"

"Actually, I moved to Dallas for a reason. I just graduated from Dallas Theological Seminary last December. I received my Master's Degree in Christian Education. But then my lease was up, my boyfriend and I had ended our relationship, and my mom had a history of falling. I thought it was time to come back to Buffalo."

"Interesting. Well that's wonderful that you came back."

As I listened, I thought of the only thing I knew about Brigham Young University: it was founded on Mormon beliefs. So most likely the family is Mormon. I felt incredibly nervous. What could I say to these people? With a house full of Mormons, could I really talk about my faith in Christ? I prayed silently, "Jesus, I believe You are with me and will give me the words."

"So, are you guys Mormon?" No reason to beat around the bush.

"Yes, we are," Cody said, "though we prefer to be called members of The Church of Jesus Christ of Latter-day Saints."

"What about you?"

"I've trusted in Jesus as my Savior, and I attend a non-denominational Christian church, The Chapel in Amherst."

"I've heard of that church. They have a fairly large congregation. We attend a Latter-day Saints church in Niagara Falls. We believe in Jesus, too; we're Christian."

This reminded me of previous conversations with Jehovah's Witnesses who claim they are Christian, but the truth reveals them to have very different views of Jesus from Christianity. I couldn't leave fundamental things unsaid. "But what do you believe about Jesus? Who is He to you?"

"He was a man, created from God. Jesus was the offspring of the Heavenly Father and a celestial wife. He was later conceived physically through intercourse between the Heavenly Father and the Virgin Mary. In the Latter-day Saint Church, Jesus is considered our elder brother."

The chatter around the table had nearly stopped. Most everyone was listening to the conversation. "So you believe Jesus was created, not present from time eternal with the Father and Holy Spirit?"

"Correct, we don't believe Jesus was always present. Joseph Smith, founder of the LDS faith, told us these things which he recorded in the Book of Mormon."

"But the Bible does tell us that Jesus has always been present, just as God the Father and the Holy Spirit. So the Book of Mormon contradicts what the Bible shows. Either the Bible—which is validated over and over—is correct or the Book of Mormon is. Both cannot be."

"We don't believe Joseph Smith taught contradictory things. The Book of Mormon was written while Joseph Smith was in the America's. Scripture is not closed, and so he wrote on tablets, what we believe later came true."

I looked at him and quoted a favorite verse. "2 Timothy 3:16 tells us that 'All Scripture is God-breathed.' As a follower of Christ, I know the Holy Spirit resides in me. If I write a book, however, that doesn't mean God authored the book, the way the Bible is completely accurate. We're also told specifically not to add or take away from the Bible or we will come under God's judgment" (Revelation 22:18).

After a lengthy discussion, we decided to delay our conversation for another time and return to the throngs of the party. I planned to pray for these new friends of mine. As I got ready to leave, Cody, Amanda, and I exchanged e-mail addresses to contact each other again.

About a month later through e-mails, Cody indicated that he visited my church on a weekday to check out the newly-built facility. Why I'm not sure, as nothing was going on that day, but I hoped that our discussions had prompted something in him.

Though we haven't seen each other in a long time, I continue to pray for Cody, Amanda, and their family. I hope they will come to the truth of Jesus as God—the uncreated Creator. They seem like nice people, but moral goodness doesn't give us a relationship with Jesus. Once we die physically, if a person believes in a different Jesus than presented to us in Scripture, then He is not our Savior, so when we face judgment for our sins, that person will go to Hell instead of Heaven. Our eternal destination is determined by our beliefs, and there is no changing our minds once we die.

Sometimes all we can be are seeds in a person's life. Though I'd like to see the fruit, I may or may not. "He has saved us and called us to a holy life—not because of anything we have done but because of His own purpose and grace. This grace was given us in Christ Jesus before the beginning of time" (2 Timothy 1:9).

Just like the little girl with the ruby lips who was more approachable one year later, I pray that over time the people I've interacted with will come to know Jesus. He is the Savior who loves them very much and wants a relationship with them now and forever.

CHAPTER 24

The Never Ending Whys

HIS HAZEL EYES LOOKED AT me with a cold stare, and then he looked away. I had given him much support for my answer. Mr. Moreland, a previous physical therapy patient-turned-friend of mine, resided at a nursing home I'd been working for a few months. I had taken a liking to many of the patients. So when I quit the position for a job at a hospital, I continued monthly or bimonthly visits to the facility. He was one of the people I frequently stopped back to see.

Oliver Moreland was in his late 70s and had Parkinson's disease. Though he was naturally tall and slim, he hunched over from his disease and had dry, papery skin on his face and arms. He scratched himself often, so he kept several bottles of creams sitting on his bedside tray and table. When he walked down the halls stooped over, he veered from one side to the other, like a steam engine that couldn't stop. He looked like he could fall at any moment. Scary.

Oliver had worked for years as an engineer and had a very strong analytical, technical personality. With a stiff face, partially from the Parkinson's disease, he rarely smiled, yet he had a dry wit about him. I had given him physical therapy when I worked for the facility, and now several friends and I regularly spent time with him. Oliver seemed to enjoy the conversations. He especially took a liking to my friend Lynda, a gregarious woman who smiled a lot and had the gift of singing. She would often take requests from Oliver and sing to him in his room.

Knowing that I, and most of the friends that visited with me were Christians, questions of faith often came up, especially around the holidays. Oliver was agnostic—basically he didn't know if there was a God or not, but he wasn't overly concerned about the thought either way.

"What happened with the island of Atlantis?" he'd ask. "Or prove to me where the Red Sea was?"

No matter what he asked, I worked hard to research it and get back to him, showing both Scriptural and archaeological or historical support. It took time, but I chose to look for answers to his questions because I really cared about Oliver. I wanted him to believe and know Jesus personally, especially given his late age. After giving him whatever support I could, at subsequent visits, I asked Oliver what he thought. Many times, instead of commenting, he would just come up with other obscure questions.

Close to a point of frustration, I decided to try a different approach. "Oliver," I asked him, "I gave you a Bible. Have you tried reading it for yourself and asking God to speak to you? He will show you the answers you are looking for. Maybe not as detailed as you want or in the timeline you are expecting, as some things are by faith, but He loves you and wants a relationship with you—now and forever."

He'd often shake his head "No" through the usual tremor he experienced from Parkinson's disease.

"Oliver, do you believe you are a sinner?"

"Yes, but so is everyone else. People often make mistakes; we are human."

"True," I said. "Just like if I broke the law for speeding or stealing, there is a penalty that has to be paid for doing those things. God is both just and merciful—either we take the judgment in Hell or Jesus does through faith in Him as Savior before we die. None of us know when our last day on earth is, only He does."

Sitting on his bed with his legs crossed, he shrugged his shoulders as if to say, "I don't care."

"All of us are getting older. Does the thought of dying scare you?"

"I'll just be dead, in the ground."

"What about your soul?" I looked at Oliver with deep concern.

"I don't think it goes anywhere. We just die like we go to sleep." He stared off into the distance.

"Oliver, God has told us through His Word that we will all end up in Heaven or Hell. You know He has provided a Savior in Jesus. When we trust in Christ, He has the power to forgive our sins and for us to spend eternity with Him! Eternity. Forever, Oliver, that's an awesome thought!"

Often during my prayer times, I thought of Oliver. "God, why, are some people so quick to believe and others not? Willful stubbornness? Has the devil blinded them? What?"

After several years of visiting Oliver and some of the other patients in the nursing home, I noticed him declining more physically. In fact, he no longer walked much. One day when we visited, his bed was made up with no Oliver in it. The nurse told us he had fallen and broken his hip. A few weeks later, Oliver returned from the hospital, but he never seemed the same after that. He couldn't walk and stayed in bed all the time. His pain and discomfort led to him taking a lot of pain medication. Lynda continued to sing to him and occasionally pray for Oliver when he allowed it.

Oliver passed away within a year of breaking his hip. Sadly, based on our previous conversations, he most likely resides in Hell now. Only God knows, though. If somehow Jesus penetrated Oliver's hard heart, he could have chosen to believe before leaving this earth. I can't answer. Only God knows Oliver's final destination.

I found his death particularly difficult—partly due to our friendship and partly because I knew about his lack of belief in Jesus. On a visit to the nursing home later on, I passed Oliver's old room as I walked down the halls. The memories remained, but I felt saddened by Oliver's lack of trust. Could I have done more, talked less, prayed more, or acted in a different way? But we must all make our own choices, and neither I nor anyone else could choose for Oliver to believe. "No one can come to me unless the Father who sent me draws them, and I will raise them up at the last day" (John 6:44).

Over the years, I felt frustrated with our debates and his "whys." To me, just endless questions from Oliver without faith in hearing the truth or wanting to firmly believe.

I describe Oliver as a man who decided to place his "why's" above faith in Jesus, who does provide answers as we earnestly seek Him. Knowing Oliver over the years showed me some of my own shortcomings, as I, too, have a "why" personality. Just like anything taken to an extreme, when you become so entangled in the next question, you may never see the answer directly in front of you. You miss sight of the big picture—that Jesus is God, that He rose from the dead, and that He gives us enough evidence to believe by faith in the eyewitness accounts in the Bible. We, too, can have eternal life with Him in Heaven when we exercise our faith.

Perhaps, when we don't understand something, it's because we don't need to yet, and God wants us to just trust Him. Maybe the answers will never be given in this life, or He'll reveal them at some point in the future. But sometimes the answers are present in God's Word as we trust in Him through our joys and adversities.

Why did the baby die at childbirth? Why is there so much injustice, poverty, suffering, and famine in the world? Some of these questions have complex answers, and some we may never find out, such as the death of a baby. But each believer must wrestle with this question on his or her own: What can we do to help others, show them Jesus, and love our neighbor as ourselves? Are we willing to step out in faith, go the extra mile, stop complaining, and become a part of the solution?

Did Oliver ever take time to "search the Scriptures" for answers to his own questions? Or did he, as we often do, merely sit back and ask, "Why?"

And consider the critical role of prayer. Seeking God, like investing in any relationship, requires time and an openness to love. When I read the Bible, I see the amazing love of God who has challenged me to change from a complete "why" person to a woman who wants to love more than I used to. That includes asking God to help me with my own problems and questions, and to guide me in areas of life, often involving other people in the process. Jesus is the Prince of Peace, sent to help a dying world. Now, instead of always asking why—I say, "Help me, God, to love and to show You to those who desperately need to know the Savior who loves them."

I asked a lot of questions about faith prior to trusting in Jesus. "Where did the pastor get that idea from?" And, "Show me in the Bible how the pastor can make those statements." From researching what I heard and studying the Bible for myself, I opened my heart and mind to hearing from God. "Faith comes by hearing and hearing by the Word of God" (Romans 10:17). No one forced me to believe or now live for Jesus—I wanted to. His answers didn't come naturally, but with some perseverance on my behalf. I slowly began to understand Scripture and apply it to my life. "Ask and it will be given to you; seek and you will find; knock and the door will be opened to you" (Matthew 7:7).

I started seeking God, and He showed me, through his Word and the help of godly teachers, little by little, that He is real and that Jesus is the truth that sets us free from the bondage of sin. He's living and can hear me. He wants a relationship with all of us, but the sad reality is, few people trust in Him. Instead they choose to trust in themselves, their material riches, and the world.

Some who question get their answers by trusting in the provider of grace, truth, love, and salvation. Others never believe and go to their grave distrusting the One Who made them.

There are many Oliver-like people out there, and, as believers, we need to listen, accept, and help if we can, but then move on to show others the growth they can have when they fully seek the God of the Bible who loves them. "For God so loved the world that he gave his one and only Son, that whoever believes in Him shall not perish but have eternal life" (John 3:16).

CHAPTER 25

Jane—His Will

FLOPPY PINK HAT, BROAD SMILE, with a twinkle in her eye, the woman sat in her wheelchair wearing a colorful summer dress. She lifted her arm and gave me a nod with her head tilted sideways.

I met Jane at a church singles' baseball game. Actually, I met her caregiver Patrick first, on the baseball field. I asked the captain of my team to place me where the balls would not fly—since I have terrible catching and throwing skills. I just like to bat.

"Left field," he told me, and there I met Patrick.

"Do you go to my church, The Chapel?" I asked, before I even knew his name.

"Yes, I attend with my patient Jane. We also go on Saturdays to B'rith Hadoshah, a Messianic Jewish Synagogue."

"I've been there before," I said. "It's the only Messianic Jewish Synagogue in the Buffalo area."

"Yes, we love it there," Patrick said, "and we enjoy going to our church on Sundays, too."

After the game, I visited with Jane. She couldn't speak verbally; instead, she used the end of a pencil to touch squares of colored letters on a word board sitting on her lap. She spelled out her words quickly to form sentences. Even though I tried to follow her hand around the board as best I could, Patrick read much faster—almost anticipating her words. Over and over we communicated as though we had known each other a very long time. That day sparked a friendship over the next several years that I will cherish for a lifetime. Jane had a zest for life and clearly demonstrated her love of Jesus. I'd never seen a wheelchair-bound person who showed such contentment despite her circumstances.

Jane contracted encephalitis at the age of twenty-two, right after graduating from college with her chemistry degree. After enduring multiple surgeries and medical treatments, she moved to the Erie County Home and Infirmary where she resided for more than twenty years. While living there, she returned to the University of Buffalo to get her master's degree. What dogged determination! For some time, Jane used her degree coding curves for the American Society for Testing and Materials (ASTM).

About six years before I met her, a grant from the State of New York allowed her to rent a single room apartment with 24-hour aide service at the Jewish Federation Apartments. This enabled her much more freedom in her comings and goings, as she had a van service that drove her to appointments and other events. When I met her at the picnic, she was about 62 years old.

Due to Jane's many physical issues, I suggested she come for outpatient physical therapy where I worked. She had received much therapy in the past, but she could benefit from a tune-up. For about six months I put her through walking, stretching, and even stair climbing exercises. Although difficult, she succeeded at short distance walking using a walker with wheels with one or two people assisting her. She got to the point where she could move around the entire lobby at the facility and navigate stairs with significant help.

Unfortunately, the carryover in her home environment did not

Patrick and Jane

happen. The aides rarely offered to walk with her or help with her exercises. I considered her exercising and walking a priority, but Jane who wanted to do many social things and go to her church, sometimes forgot to do them.

One Christmas season, after I had discharged her from physical therapy at the hospital, Patrick and Jane asked if I would like to help them deliver Hanukkah gifts to the residents in her building. They had done this sometimes several times a year near the Jewish Holidays. Thinking it wouldn't require a huge commitment, I agreed. I didn't know the extent of the operation Jane had set up—boxes full of plastic bags surrounded her kitchen. Each bag contained some candy, a Merry Christmas and a Happy Hanukkah note, and a list of the times of services at the Messianic Jewish Synagogue.

For the next two weekends, I helped Jane and Patrick ring doorbells and deliver these gifts. Many Jewish immigrants from Russia lived in the building and Patrick could converse with them as he knew the language from having lived there for two years doing missions work. I loved helping Jane and Patrick with these deliveries. Sometimes the people invited us in for tea. Other times no one answered the door—although you could hear a television in the background. Still others simply just took the bag and quickly shut the door. Jane's heart seemed so pure, in that she regularly prayed for lost people. Despite her limited abilities, she allowed God to use her for His glory as His ambassador in a world where most physical and speech disabilities are looked upon as ruining lives. She saw her challenges as temporary disabilities until she saw her Savior in Heaven. Instead she brought life to people—through her unwavering trust in Jesus.

She had her flaws like all of us do. Very persistent in what she wanted, she was hard to slow down. But her persistence had advantages, too. She never quit showing others that Jesus is the Messiah. On the back of her electric, a bumper sticker read, "Pray for the peace of Jerusalem." On her manual wheelchair the sticker said, "My Father is a Jewish Carpenter."

One day she e-mailed me that her aide, Kim had trusted in Jesus as her Savior. Jane prayed and shared the Gospel with Kim for several years. God blessed Jane by allowing her to see a life truly transformed.

On Sundays, Jane and her aide for that day, would sit in the front of the church near the pastor's wife, Edie. With all her strength Jane would lift her right arm in tune to the music, praising God with a broad smile on her face. At times though, I'd see her dozing off during the service from all the medications she took.

Nothing seemed to discourage her. Despite her intense physical infirmities, as long as she could get there, she attended services every Saturday and Sunday, along with many other events—singles' and women's Bible studies. She also attended Western New York Apologetic Meetings, and she took classes at the University of Buffalo. At Darien Lake Amusement Park, at the Kingdom

Bound Christian Music Festival, Patrick shocked me by lifting Jane onto the rides. We all rode the Ferris wheel together. She beamed with joy!

When I looked at Jane, I saw a woman in a wheelchair with her neck bent sideways, orthopedic scars from multiple surgeries, and finger deformities, yet she still held out one arm for a hug. She needed others for her physical care of course, but she really was a strong, independent woman. She enjoyed people and relied on the Lord as her rock of faith.

After I had known Jane for a while, I saw deeper qualities—a will of steel, so much love for the Lord and others, and a special quality of excitement that you wanted to inhale. When someone asked her how she was doing, she usually wrote on her board, "I'm blessed and highly favored by the Lord."

Things just didn't get her down much except when someone didn't believe in Jesus or fell ill—then I would see her tears flowing in buckets. God's always in control, and Jane seemed to know that, yet as a human being she showed her deep feelings, as well.

Jane acted as my spiritual mentor, someone I could go to for godly advice and wisdom. "Jane," I would ask, "what do you think I should do about this...?"

She almost always gave me time despite many friends who flocked around her to give a hug and talk with her. Jane was a very close friend of mine, not because she had all the answers, but because of her genuineness. She offered me great encouragement in learning to walk by faith, even though she couldn't physically walk!

Several times, I would get phone calls on Sunday mornings via a relay system.

"Pam the van isn't coming, could you kindly pick me up?" Always with manners, Jane never forgot to say please and thank you even if it did take more time to communicate.

My feelings told me what an inconvenience it would cause as

I had to get her out of the wheelchair, transfer her into my SUV, and load her wheelchair and bags of medical supplies she needed for her PEG tube feedings through her stomach. Her nurse's aide would accompany us in my vehicle, too.

Nearly every time Jane asked for a ride, I said yes, unless she called extremely late in the morning. The result was always the same—I felt so blessed! For the extra time and trouble needed to get her anywhere, she was such a joy to be around and a fellow sister in Christ who I served for the glory of the King.

At one point, Jane got very sick and stayed in the hospital for over a month. I ran up to see her on my lunch breaks and after work. I looked at her communication board while I stroked her hair, moistened with sweat. Most people would not have the same frequently used words she had printed on her board—Hallelujah, PTL for "Praise the Lord," Joy, and many others that referred to God Who gave her the strength she needed through adversity.

"God," I prayed silently, "only if it be Your will, take her. She is such a good friend and, for my own selfish reasons, I don't want her to leave this earth yet. Please heal her."

Eventually God did heal her, but not the way I hoped for. Jane left this earth for a new home—one where she will live with Jesus forever, in Heaven. Finally out of her wheelchair and with a new heavenly body, I'm sure she's as active as ever and singing in perfect pitch to the King of Kings and Lord of Lords.

Jane's strong and determined will taught me, and countless others—to live every day for Jesus. She shined her light pointing others to Him. It's easy to thank God when things go well, but to see someone praise Him when life had dealt them such a difficult hand—being unable to speak or move very freely—only with Christ in us is that possible!

CHAPTER 26

Accidents That Bring Change

AFTER A NIGHT OF DRINKING, Adam stumbled around the middle of the road around four o'clock in the morning. A driver that couldn't see him, hit him at a fast speed. Adam had a scar that looked like tire tread on his torso. Adam is about 6'4" and lanky, and he has medium-brown hair cut in a military style.

Adam started seeing me for outpatient physical therapy after his accident. He came into the clinic twice a week. I gave Adam a series of exercises to help relieve his complaints of hip pain, and he used several pieces of equipment in the gym area.

As we got to know each other, Adam asked what made me decide on a career as a physical therapist.

"I watched my mom pass out after a dental procedure and fall down the basement steps. She broke her arm in three places. Though she had surgery on it, she still suffered a tremendous amount of pain. Seeing the intense therapy she went through, I found the profession interesting. I graduated with my degree in physical therapy so I could work with people like you Adam."

He nodded while continuing to do his leg exercises.

"I enjoy helping people. But I prefer to help people in ways besides working as a therapist."

"What do you mean?"

"So many people don't believe in Christ. I want everyone to know Him as their Lord and Savior. That pursuit means even more to me than assisting someone with a physical problem."

"I never believed in God," he said, "until this accident. Now I know there's a God."

"A friend of mine thought like that. She remained in a coma for two days from a motorcycle accident. When she came out of it, she wanted to know more about Jesus, when before she wanted no part of Him. Sometimes accidents bring more than physical changes. When you were growing up did your family ever talk about God?" I asked.

"No, and we never went to church. But ever since my accident, I decided I'm going to look for a church."

"Do you believe in Jesus?" I asked.

"I don't know." His look told me he had many questions.

A few conversations later, I boldly asked, "Adam, I brought a few things for you about Jesus. Would you like them? You don't have to take them if you don't want to."

"Sure, I'll take them."

I handed him two small paperbacks, *The Gospel of John* and *More Than a Carpenter* by Josh McDowell. "You can keep them," I said.

The following two weeks I had a lot of patients, so Adam and I had minimal conversations during his physical therapy sessions.

As we neared the end of his prescribed physical therapy, I commended him on his progress. "Your balance and strength are better, but you're still complaining of pain. I'll have to discharge you from therapy soon, and you'll need to see the doctor for further evaluation."

"Ok, I understand. You know I haven't read those books you gave me yet, but I've thought a lot about what we've talked about."

As I watched Adam walk out the clinic door late that Friday afternoon, I felt like I should have said more. Now I've lost that opportunity, I thought.

About five minutes later, as I started to turn the lights off to leave for the day, the door opened, and Adam walked in. "Hey Pam, I forgot something. Can you stamp my parking ticket?"

I stamped the ticket and handed it back to him. "I also wanted to ask you something, if you don't mind."

"Go ahead."

"Would you like to talk about Jesus now?"

He paused for a second and said, "Yeah, I would like that."

My heart pounded, and I felt my eyes light up. "Do you have some time? Maybe we can go through the Bible a little."

"Sure, I'm not in a hurry." He pulled over one of the clinic chairs and sat down.

I retrieved my Bible from my desk. Years before, I wrote out Romans Road on the inside cover for evangelism purposes—verses that show the way to salvation through Jesus using the book of Romans.

I wanted to make sure that Adam really understood that Jesus is God and what it means to trust in Him. I led him through the verses of Romans Road, and Adam read each one aloud. After the last verse, I asked him, "Are you ready to trust in Jesus?"

"Yes," he said with a smile and gleam in his eyes.

"Adam, let's pray." We closed our eyes and Adam repeated the words after I spoke.

"Jesus, I'm a sinner. I believe you died for my sins and rose again from the dead. I repent of my sins and disbelief, and I trust in You alone as my Savior. Please forgive me of all of my sins. I will spend eternity with you in Heaven, and You'll be with me while on earth now. Thank you for forgiving me. I will try to follow you all the days of my life. In Jesus' name, Amen."

Adam looked up at me with a smile of satisfaction and peace. "Thanks Pam. I'm really glad we did that."

"I'm happy for you!" I hugged him and welcomed him to the family of believers. Before he left, I encouraged him to find a good Bible-believing church.

The following week I discharged Adam from physical therapy. I pray God continues to transform his character and that he grows closer to the Lord.

Romans Road

- **We need salvation found only in Jesus as Savior—no matter how "good" we think we are. Every human is sinful, God is holy.**
  Romans 3:10—As it is written, "There is no one righteous, not even one.

- **The punishment we have earned for our sins is both physical and eternal death.**
  Romans 6:23—For the wages of sin is death, but the gift of God is eternal life in Christ Jesus our Lord.

- **Jesus Christ proved His love by dying on the cross for us. We deserve His death paid the price of our sins.**
  Romans 5:8—But God demonstrates his own love for us in this: While we were still sinners, Christ died for us.

- **If you believe in who Jesus is—Lord, and that He died on the cross and defeated death, you too will be saved from your sins and spend eternity one day in Heaven.**
  Romans 10:9-10—If you declare with your mouth, "Jesus is Lord," and believe in your heart that God raised him from the dead, you will be saved. For it is with your heart that you believe and are justified, and it is with your mouth that you profess your faith and are saved.

- **Jesus died to pay the penalty for our sins and rescue us from an eternity in Hell. Forgiveness of sins is available to anyone who trusts in Jesus Christ as their Lord and Savior.**
Romans 10:13—for, "Everyone who calls on the name of the Lord will be saved.

Example of a prayer after reading Roman's Road, knowing that it's not the words that save you, only your belief in Jesus Christ as your Savior:

"God, I know that I am a sinner and I deserve death—Hell. I believe that Jesus Christ died on a cross as payment for my punishment. I turn from any disbelief I've had and I turn from my sin. I trust alone in Jesus as my Lord and Savior. Thank You God for your forgiveness, grace, and giving me eternal life with You in Heaven. Amen."

CHAPTER 27

Jewish by Tradition

"DO YOU WANT TO GO horseback riding with us?"

I laughed out loud at the thought. "What? You're my patients."

"That's okay, we don't care; come with us this weekend."

I treated Ned and Suzette in the physical therapy clinic for their knee and back problems. I had seen them for only a few sessions prior to their asking. I enjoyed their personalities and their sense of humor. A sweet couple, they complimented each other. Suzette, usually laughing and quite vivacious, had quick spontaneous comments. Her asking me to go horseback riding was no exception.

Ned was a little more reserved, but he maintained a calm, friendly demeanor. Both were retired from the Air Force and in their early sixties. Ned taught religion at a local college. He was also a Jewish Rabbi, which I learned during one of our discussions as I treated his knee.

Ned applied his own gentle pressure to get me to say yes. "Come on Pam, you'll have fun. We have three horses—one is a foal, but the other two we ride frequently. We'll see you Saturday, okay?"

How could I refuse such a persuasive invitation? "Sure, I

look forward to it, even though I don't have much riding experience. I've only gone horseback riding maybe four times in my life, on slow horses."

"That's fine; we'll give you lessons."

That Saturday I met Ned and Suzette at the riding stables. They planned to give me English horseback riding lessons. Something I also knew nothing about. They taught me how to approach and get on their horse—a beautiful, velvety brown one named Chocolate. They adjusted the stirrups and demonstrated how to hold the reins to direct Chocolate. They instructed me on how to use my voice and legs to get the horse to move faster or stop.

The day went quickly, and after my riding lessons ended, we went to a local mall restaurant for Chinese food. I wanted to get to know Ned and Suzette both as friends to hang out with and also because they were Jewish. I cared about their souls—where they spent eternity—as they didn't believe in Jesus.

They had both grown-up in the Midwest and met in high school. Eventually their military careers brought them to the Buffalo area. They never had any children, but they had their horses and other animals.

When their physical therapy treatments with me ended, we stayed in contact. One year they asked me to come to a Seder with Ned's congregation. Detailed in the book of Exodus, the Passover Seder celebrates the liberation of the Israelites from slavery in Egypt. At first I didn't know if going to this service was okay, since I'm a follower of Jesus. I asked my pastor, who said, since Jews do believe in the Old Testament of the Bible, there was no reason I couldn't go.

A few weeks later, I drove the hour to arrive at their Reform Jewish synagogue. Nervous, I prayed the whole time, asking

Jesus to show them that He is the Messiah the Jewish people have waited for. I sat at a long table, next to cousins of Ned and Suzette's. As the dinner progressed, I tried to bring up spiritual topics. The man next to me, Reuben, said that he didn't believe in God and attended the Seder for tradition only.

That burdened my heart, so many people not believing in the Lord. I knew the Jewish population was generally made up of non-believers, less than 1% of the estimated fifteen million Jews in the world are Messianic—have come to faith in Jesus as the Messiah. Yet, reflecting on the people at the Seder service made me want to talk to them even more about Jesus, known by the Hebrew name Yeshua, who had come to save people from their sins and bring them everlasting life.

While walking around the room after dinner, I met Patti, a woman of small stature who had shoulder-length dark hair. She was in her late twenties and studied nursing at a nearby college. When Ned showed me around the synagogue, Patti went with me to see the Torah Scroll that Ned took out from a cabinet called the "aron kodesh" (holy cabinet) to show us.

Afterwards, Patti talked to me about growing up Roman Catholic, her disassociation with it, and her new love for the Jewish faith, to which she converted to a few years ago. I asked her if she had looked into Messianic Judaism—Jews who believe in Jesus as the Messiah. She said she had not. Just before I left for the night, we exchanged phone numbers.

I contacted Patti and invited her to my church, and she came. I also tried to share with her about the fulfillment of the prophecies in the Old Testament—the Torah, and how they came true in the New Testament. I lent her a book on Messianic Judaism. Patti seemed extremely busy working two jobs and attending college. Over the course of about a year and a half, we lost touch.

After meeting Ned and Suzette at their gym one day to work-out, we grabbed a light bite to eat at the café there, where we got into a discussion of their beliefs. They truly didn't believe Jesus was the Messiah.

I shared with them a few things I'd considered about the topic. "If I was born in a Jewish household, what characteristics would I look for in the Messiah? How would I know who He is? After looking through the Tanukh—the Old Testament, I see multiple prophecies. Micah 5:2 showed that the Messiah would be born in Bethlehem Ephrathah, which we see took place (Matthew 2:1). He would be called Immanuel, 'God with us' (Isaiah 7:14 fulfilled in Matthew 1:23). Betrayed for thirty pieces of silver (Zechariah 11:12, fulfilled in Matthew 26:14-15).

Overall, there are more than three hundred prophecies or predictions written hundreds of years before the coming Messiah which Jesus fulfilled (Jeremiah 31:31). This overwhelming evidence points clearly to Jesus being God. The Bible shows me, that God in His human form, Jesus, can be trusted. God gives us evidence through the Bible of where the Messiah will be born, of what familial ancestry, born of a virgin, the miracles He performed, and how He would die. With that kind of proof, we can believe Jesus is God and trust Him as our Savior."

As for Ned and Suzette, our discussions have continued, but unfortunately, I haven't seen much direct change in their beliefs. They have heard the Gospel several times at my church services and also at church plays. God is faithful, and even though we may not see a difference, He hears us and knows when our hearts are pure asking for wisdom and guidance in life. Praying to God for salvation of friends and family, and for more workers of the harvest, is in harmony with His will. Only God, however, knows if they will ever come to faith in Jesus. God did not create robots. He blesses each of us with free will and with that comes the responsibility and consequences of obedience and living a righteous life—not perfect, but with God in control. The opposite can also happen—a lack of faith and commitment to the one true God who made them.

Jesus came for everyone, Jews and Gentiles alike, to believe. When I think of friends like Ned and Suzette, who have not trusted in Him yet, I think of people who are not walking by the faith of the Bible the Lord has given us. They continue to lean on the crutch of their traditions. Instead, Jews would do better to explore how the roots of those traditions lead to the coming of the Messiah and the redemption of the Jewish people through Jesus.

The Messiah, Jesus, doesn't want them to think culturally, but relationally. He is present in the world now; He's waiting for them to trust and receive Him, in order to reconcile them to the Father. When Jesus spoke to some cultural Jews that did not believe in Him, He said, "You know neither me nor my Father. If you knew me, you would know my Father also" (John 8:19).

The Bible states, "But their minds were made dull, for to this day the same veil remains when the old covenant is read. It has not been removed, because only in Christ is it taken away" (2 Corinthians 3:14). The majority of Jewish people cannot understand that their minds are veiled and their hearts hardened. They don't see that the Mosaic ministry has ended and the New Covenant, fulfilled in Jesus, has arrived.

If Ned and Suzette and all my other non-believing family and friends trust in Jesus before they die, I would love that. We would spend eternity together in Heaven. What a blessing to live forever with Jesus and all the other believers in a beautiful, perfect place. Yet I know the reality of Jesus' preaching on Hell, which He spoke more about than love. Only God knows the future of a person's life, and we need to faithfully show our belief in Jesus in words and actions.

Note

About eight years after I had last spoken to Patti, I went to Congregation B'rith Hadoshah Messianic Synagogue for Erev Rosh Hashanah (the day before Rosh Hashanah—one of the High Holy Days). I went with my friend Sandy, a non-believing Jewish lady.

After the service was over, they had many tables of scrumptious deserts and coffee. As I walked over to grab a cup of coffee, I heard someone calling, "Pam, Pam." I turned and there stood Patti! She came up to me and asked, "Do you remember me?"

"Of course I remember you." I smiled broadly.

"I'm here because of you. Do you remember when you gave me that book on Jesus and told me about Messianic Judaism and B'rith Hadoshah?"

"Yes, of course." My mind traveled back to those days.

"Well, I thought a lot about what we talked about and what I read from that book about Jesus being the Messiah. Then for almost three years I was engaged to a Jewish man, who said it was not Jewish to believe in Jesus. He would not allow me to come to the Messianic Synagogue. I knew he was wrong, so I finally ended the relationship. As soon as I did, I started coming to B'rith Hadoshah and have been attending here ever since. I wouldn't be here if it hadn't been for you."

"Patti, it wasn't me; it was the Holy Spirit, but I'm so happy that you have been coming. Have you trusted in Jesus as your Savior?"

"Yes, of course, I have."

We talked a little longer, and Patti gave me her new phone number to keep in touch.

Sandy, me, and Ana at my birthday party

This night felt like such a wonderful blessing to me from the Lord. All those years later, I always wondered what happened with Patti. God showed me through this experience, even if we get discouraged and wonder if our sharing Christ with others is ever going to produce fruit, just keep doing it! He is the only one Who saves people, but we have the privilege of participating in the process of someone knowing the Lord.

Sandy decided at the end of the evening that although she wasn't a believer yet, she had questions. "I don't know if I could ever change," she said. "I'm seventy-seven."

I've known Sandy for over ten years. She has come to my church, as well as B'rith Hadoshah several times and has heard about Jesus at other functions including Christian movies. Years ago, I also gave her a Bible and encouraged her to read it.

"You're still here on this earth, Sandy. The only way you will find the truth is to seek God. Look at the Scriptures about who the Messiah is. He actually says He is the truth. No one is going to force you to believe in Jesus. I truly care about you and want you to know Him, but you have to make the choice and decide on your beliefs. And making no decision to believe in Him, is to not believe in who Jesus says He is."

The following Saturday I picked up Sandy and we went to the Torah study after the Shabbot service at the Messianic Synagogue. I ran into Patti there again. Wonderful, I thought, how God blesses me by helping others to possibly know Him one day. I pray that Sandy also would put her trust in Jesus as her Lord and Savior, before it's too late.

CHAPTER 28

Fairs to Remember

IF SOMEONE TOLD ME YEARS ago that I would spend time doing evangelism at a state fair, I would have said, "You're crazy, why would I do that? It sounds more like fear evangelism." But that's exactly what happened. In my mid-thirties, after trusting in Christ about ten years prior, I attended Dallas Theological Seminary. Often we received notices in our school mailbox of various ministries we could get involved in. One day, I received a request for volunteers to work in a booth sharing about Jesus at the Texas State Fair.

Since childhood, I've loved attending fairs—county, state, it didn't matter. I always have fun at them. Not that I was a country bumpkin, but I enjoyed the many things they offered—food, animals, rides, vending tables, even taking some health-related tests. What a variety of things to do!

So after seeing the notice at seminary, I called the number and signed up for evangelism at the fair. I had shared the Gospel of Jesus before, more one on one with someone I knew, even if briefly such as at an event. But this would involve conversations with complete strangers, so I felt a little nervous. I blocked the apprehension out of my mind. I wanted people to know the Lord, and that desire triumphed over any lack of courage. God would want me to love people as He would—through sharing His Word.

When I arrived at the fair, there were already a few workers in the booth. We discussed several ways for bringing up the subject of Jesus. The day went pretty smoothly, and I listened and observed as several people prayed to trust in Christ. The man who ran the booth, Jimmy, did fair evangelism all over the country throughout the warm months. He set up a cot behind the back curtain wall to take naps. I felt a little sorry for him. Considering all the work he put in, that cot certainly wasn't a plush way to take a snooze. Yet, he was doing something that mattered to him and the Lord, and I could see that he enjoyed the fruits of his labor—seeing lives changed for the glory of God.

In Buffalo, New York, several years later, I also did evangelism at the Erie County Fair. I told a friend, Frank, about my upcoming plans, and although he admitted to being nervous, he wanted to go, too. A few weeks before the fair, we went for a night of training with both seasoned veterans and those who had never shared Jesus. During the training we learned to get the main points of the Gospel across and not to focus on more trivial matters. Ralph, who had done fair evangelism for over 22 years, and his pastor instructed us. The Gospel presentation was based on Biblical principles, to show why we need a Savior as the solution for our sin.

The first day I went, Ralph was also in the booth with me. As I sat on a stool behind the counter, I watched a heavy woman, about fifty, read the posted sign asking, 'Do you know if you are going to Heaven?' The dark-haired woman then approached me.'

"Hi, my name's Pam. What's your name?"

"Anita," she said.

"Can I ask you a question?" I said to the woman.

"Sure, go ahead."

"Do you know for sure, without a shadow of a doubt, that you will go to Heaven?"

"Yes, I think so," she said.

"Can I ask you why you think you would go to Heaven?"

"Because I'm a pretty good person, I try to live by the golden rule. I haven't murdered anyone or done anything really bad."

"Can I share what the Bible states?"

"Go ahead," she said. "I'm listening."

"Romans 3:23 states, 'For all have sinned and fallen short of the glory of God.' That means every one of us is a sinner. We all have that in common, right? Perhaps we've told a lie, stolen something even small, lusted after someone, or taken the Lord's name in vain. The point is we are all sinners."

Anita nodded her head, yes, in agreement.

"The second thing is the Bible says, 'The wages of sin is death, but the gift of God is eternal life.' Now a wage is something we receive for what we do. God says what we earn for our sin is separation from Him, in Hell. Why? Because He is a just God and must punish those who break His laws. But the Good News is, Jesus died on the cross, and His death took those wages and punishment for us. Now we can choose to pay our own debt, if we like, or we can accept what Christ has done for us. Quite frankly I'd much rather accept what He did for me, wouldn't you?"

"Yes," Anita mouthed.

"And number three, the Bible also states that 'whosoever calls upon the name of the Lord shall be saved.' Whosoever means anyone can."

"So before you go, can I pray for you Anita?"

I extended my hand, and she took it. I prayed for God to bless Anita and her family with a long and healthy life. I asked Jesus to make Himself very real to her. "And Anita," I said, "if you have never received Jesus Christ as your Lord and Savior I pray that you would do so right now. If you, too, would like to receive Jesus Christ as your Lord and Savior, just say this after me..."

"You can repeat something like this: 'Dear Lord Jesus, I know I'm a sinner and I'm sorry for my sins. I believe Jesus died on the cross to pay my debt, to take my wages. Right now, please come into my heart, and forgive my sins. I accept You as my personal Lord and Savior. I thank you that my sins are now forgiven and I'm on my way to Heaven. In Jesus' name. Amen.'"

"If you sincerely meant that prayer, just give my hand a squeeze."

Anita gave my hand a good squeeze. Tears welled up in my eyes when Anita trusted in Jesus. I felt excited for her as she was now in a relationship with the Creator of the universe. Only God knows whether she truly meant what she prayed, but I pray God continues to work in her life. As the Scriptures showed us, our good deeds can never get us to Heaven; only our faith in what Jesus did for us on the cross can do that. Anita previously had trusted in her own works to get to Heaven, but only God is perfect and has the ability to forgive sins when we repent and trust in Him.

"Anita, do you have a church you can attend?"

She said she did not, so I asked her where she lived and gave her a list of Bible-believing churches in that area. I also encouraged her to read the Bible and pray daily to seek God. Just like spending time with your best friend, spending time with God results in you knowing Him better and you develop more Christ-like characteristics.

During one of the days I spent in the booth, Emma, a woman about twenty, trusted in Jesus. Afterwards, without provocation, she immediately took off the shirt she was wearing. She had on another one underneath, I hadn't noticed, but it read "Gay Pride." Emma's friend stood nearby, with her arms crossed looking mad, but it didn't matter. If Emma really surrendered to Jesus, just like taking off the shirt, her actions would follow Him. When we accept His gift of grace and mercy, and choose to live for Him, He changes not only our outsides, but also our insides.

Years ago, I modeled part-time doing fashion, runway, and promotional shows. Often I did it for myself only because I wanted to look good on the outside in the clothes and makeup. I liked the attention of people and the camera. I saw the extra money as a perk, too. I realized later those feelings were short-lived. Now, it felt much better on the inside, helping someone else who couldn't pay me back, such as a patient at work, or someone like Emma and Anita who need Jesus. The eternal consequences of seeing someone in Heaven one day, compared to being separated from Jesus in Hell, is a monumental reward to me—something like love, that money can't buy.

God has changed me over the years, but it's funny how He still manages to orchestrate my likes and desires to fit into the story for my life. Because, you see, my story is so much better when He runs my life, not Pam.

CHAPTER 29

Crohn's Disease Gone!

"I NEED TO GO HOME now," I said.

"Now? In the middle of dinner?" Frank asked.

"Yes, my stomach is killing me." I clenched my arms across my abdomen under the table. I walked out of the restaurant holding my stomach, reclined the seat of the truck and lay there uncomfortably.

After getting home, I writhed in pain on the living room floor. I take care of my mom who has Parkinson's Disease. She has physical problems but is completely "with it."

Sitting in her recliner, she saw me lying there. "Pam, what is wrong with you?"

"I don't know. My stomach hurts really bad."

"You'd better go to Immediate Care or the ER."

"I'm not going," I said. "It's probably the flu or something."

Over the next month, my stomach pains continued. I went to work every day and often wore my lab coat over my usual clothes, with my pants loosened. When I walked, I constantly wanted to lean forward from the pain. During lunch, I often shut the door and rested on a mat table in one of the treatment rooms.

Eventually, I realized this stomach issue wasn't relenting so

I knocked on the office door of a doctor I knew at the hospital I worked at.

"Do I have the flu?" I asked, "My stomach pain has been going on for almost a month. I have sores in my mouth too, and I've never had those."

"Honey, you don't have the flu," the doctor said. "Go up to the GI clinic and have them look at you."

I went upstairs to the clinic and made the earliest appointment I could get with a gastroenterologist—two days away. That night, after getting home, I couldn't stand the pain again and ended up in the ER. After laying there all night, they finally did a CAT scan of my abdomen and gave me morphine. Of course, the morphine helped the pain, but I felt quite woozy. By the next day, the morphine had worn off, and the pain had returned.

Within a few weeks, after many more tests, my GI doctor confirmed the diagnosis of Crohn's disease, ileocolitis.

"How can I have that?" I said. "I thought people get Crohn's when they are eighteen or nineteen?"

"You can get it at any time in your life, Pam," the doctor said. "I have one patient who is eighty-three and just diagnosed with it."

"What can I do for it? When will it go away?"

"Pills," she said.

"For how long?"

"The rest of your life. People do not get off them. It's a chronic condition—an autoimmune disorder and systemic. That's why you have the mouth sores. Once you start taking the medication, it should help soon. But you cannot go off the pills; to do so could cause very serious problems."

Could she tell me anything worse, I thought, as I made my way out of the building and cried in my car. And it doesn't go away, so I'll have it for the rest of my life? I started envisioning

Family Circus © 2013 Bil Keane Inc. Dist by King Features Syndicate, Inc.

surgeries, a colostomy bag, and all the bad things that could potentially happen.

I filled the prescription for the medication and began taking it immediately, Pentasa, 500 mg, 8 pills/day. Within a week, I felt great, pain-free, like I was in Heaven. Back to myself—almost. Three months later though, the pain started returning severely. I felt no relief. They put me on another drug that's used for chemotherapy patients.

In the meantime, I decided to go with the women's ministry of my church on a mission trip to Costa Rica. No sense in sitting around all the time, I thought, just being sick.

The trip was great, but my health was an issue. I had to lie down a lot and the chemotherapy drug made me feel sick to my stomach. I took heavier doses of pain pills, which helped a little, but in time the effects from those wore off, too.

When I got back to Buffalo, I started going to support group meetings for Crohn's. There wasn't much to change in my diet other than going from skim to almond milk. I also tried to eat more slowly, which was difficult for me as I'm generally a fast-paced person. My doctor explained that I had pockets in my intestines, which means if you eat too quickly, the food almost gets stuck, like in a narrow funnel. Many foods could make my pain worse, especially raw vegetables and green salads, which I always liked. Although my weight didn't change much, I became anemic (low red blood cells) despite iron supplements. Since I couldn't eat green leafy vegetables to help my anemia and I ate a lot of mashed potatoes, I thought why not steak! The doctor got a kick out of how I improved my lab values by eating one or two steaks every day.

Despite the mild dietary changes I made, the years challenged both my physical and mental health. I often felt like I had cancer. I barely made it through work and sometimes went home sick. When I got home, I rested on the couch or the carpeted floor clutching my stomach in agony. The only thing that really helped was lying still and not eating anything. Unfortunately, this "treatment" gave my insides a rest, but it took a long time—sometimes up to eight to ten hours. I tried multiple suggestions such as peppermint tea and ginger. I rubbed peppermint oil on my stomach, but any improvement was very short-lived.

My social life definitely changed. I couldn't make a lot of events, or I would get there and leave because I didn't feel well. I remember going to a friend's wedding and having such unbearable pain, I spent most of the evening in the car with the seat reclined trying to get my pain to calm down. The doctor said I could try other medications, but after going to the support groups and hearing the side effects and the stories of multiple surgeries, it scared me. So I just kept taking the current regimen. During this time, thankfully I had close friends and my church that prayed for me, and my family who encouraged me.

Stress could make my pain worse, but I found laughter did help somewhat. You can't tell someone having a heart attack, "Just laugh and everything will go away." However, since my pain was generally constant and not an emergency, telling jokes and having fun especially when the pain was not overly acute, helped. I often think of the verse, "A cheerful heart is good medicine, but a crushed spirit dries up the bones" (Proverbs 17:22). There's a lot of wisdom packed in that verse.

In January, I decided to work on another problem. My back and right leg had bothered me for some time due to a lumbar disc bulge or herniation. I had many of those in the past, but they'd always healed. This disc problem didn't seem to want to change despite the many, many physical therapy exercises I did and going to a chiropractor multiple times. Most of the time, however the stomach pain outweighed the back and leg pain, so I didn't focus on it.

On a Monday night, I volunteered my physical therapy services at Good Neighbors Health Care, an outreach center on the east side of Buffalo which offers free medical care to the community. The doctors, nurses, and other medical personnel always pray for the patients prior to the start of treatments. I asked if they could pray for my back and leg as it bothered me a lot that evening. I told them how I had tried nearly everything I could think of to help improve my condition—physical therapy, chiropractic care, working out, swimming, medications, and definitely prayer.

One of the doctors asked if I had tried acupuncture. "No," I said, "Maybe I will try that."

The doctor suggested acupuncture so I looked up someone he

recommended. I decided I didn't want to go to him because he had a lot of New Age philosophies. I then researched acupuncture on Christian websites; I wanted to see if getting acupuncture would in any way violate my conscience as a believer in Christ. Acupuncture can help certain painful conditions and has rational scientific evidence for it. However, it's extremely important that the practitioner you choose doesn't try to influence you into the bondage of false Eastern religions. (http://www.gotquestions.org/acupuncture-Christian.html)

The following weekend, I had lunch with two friends. I told them about how the doctor from Good Neighbors thought acupuncture might help my back and leg symptoms.

"Why don't you try going to John Wingfield?" Sue said. "He goes to our church, and he's a Christian and a nurse. He and his wife, Stacie, have gone on vacation with my husband and me. He's a very nice man; I think you'll like him."

I called John and went over to his house for a treatment the following weekend. Before I walked in, I prayed in my car, "Lord, if this treatment is not for me, make it very clear soon."

John was quite thorough and detailed about how he does acupuncture. When John asked me my medical history, I told him about my Crohn's disease and colitis. "Would you mind if I treat your stomach as well?" he asked.

"Go right ahead; use the biggest needles you have. I want everything gone."

Twenty-eight needles later, I left. That week, I noticed something amazing. No stomach pain. My back and leg were the same though.

I called John, ecstatic. In the past year, every day I woke up I felt stomach pain, anywhere from mild to severe, even while taking pain medications. I spent far too much time in the bathroom—sometimes going ten times before walking out the door to go to work. My energy was sapped. But after the prayer and treatment from John, I felt great—like I could walk on air.

The pain started coming back a little, so I went for two more sessions with John. Each time he prayed to Jesus and then performed the acupuncture. I continued feeling better.

Two months after the three treatments with John, I got the flu. It seemed strange. One week I felt sick, the next week, I'd feel fine. Yet, it continued. Several times after leaving work, I pulled over and threw up on the side of the road.

I finally left work one afternoon to see my primary doctor. "Pam," my primary doctor said. "You can't have the flu for a month."

"Then why am I throwing up?" I asked.

"We will do CAT scan of abdomen," he said in his Indian accent.

As I waited two hours to have the test done, I looked through magazines and newspapers in the clinic, as I hadn't brought any reading material with me. I read the comics. One in particular stuck out to me. Family Circus showed a little boy praying with a caption, "How do I know God hears my prayers, when I just say 'em in my head?"

Yes, I thought, that's how I've sometimes felt these past few years since my diagnosis of Crohn's. Many, many people—including me—have prayed asking God to take away this disease and heal my intestines. God, are you listening? I knew He heard our prayers, yet no action. But today was different. I felt like God spoke to my heart at that moment: "This will happen."

I wasn't 100% sure if that was my imagination, since I desperately wanted healing of my Crohn's disease, or truly the Holy Spirit. I cut the cartoon out of the newspaper and put it in my purse.

After the CAT scan, my primary doctor called me back into the office and said, "Pam, there is no evidence of Crohn's, no scarring whatsoever. I want you to go to another GI doctor."

"That's great news! I'm glad. I don't know why I've been throwing up, but the pain from my Crohn's has not been there."

It took another month to get in to see another GI doctor, Dr. Grant. I told him how my stomach had been feeling much better since January when I saw John who prayed for me and gave me three acupuncture treatments. I also told him the results of the recent CAT scan. Dr. Grant said he wasn't so sure my diagnosis of Crohn's was accurate. He planned on repeating all the tests and getting my previous tests and reexamining those. He told me it was my choice if I wanted to continue with my current meds or I could stop taking them. About two weeks later, I gradually went off the pills without any side effects.

After completing the tests, including a colonoscopy, I saw Dr. Grant again.

"Pam, I reviewed your previous tests, along with a top colleague of mine who I very much respect. We both agree, you definitely had Crohn's Disease. When I saw the results of your recent tests, comparing them to the past ones, it was like looking at two different people."

"Am I in remission?"

"No, if you were in remission there would be scarring. You have no evidence of Crohn's disease or colitis anymore."

"Wow, Dr. Grant, that's great! Jesus does heal, and He used John and everyone else, even you Dr. Grant."

"I don't know if He used me Pam."

"I do, Dr. Grant, I believe."

"Well, I'm going to order one more test, to see if you have any evidence of irritable bowel syndrome. You did fail the hydrogen breath test, and if you want, I can put you on a short course of antibiotics."

"Sure go ahead. I'm just so glad, as this has been an extremely tough experience."

Upon leaving the doctor's office, I started crying for much of the evening and next morning—tears of joy this time. God did hear my prayers. I thought of how over the years, each time I saw my original GI doctor, she would tell me this disease would never go away. My response was always the same. "I respect you as a doctor, but…if God wants to heal me and give me a miracle, He will."

It's always His choice whether He ultimately heals people, as we often don't understand when He doesn't. No matter how much medical care and responsibility we take for trying to do all the "right" things, the final outcome is in His hands. It's His will be done, as the Lord's Prayer says.

It's easy to trust when things are going great, but when they aren't, we tend to wonder, "Don't you care God?" But I know from reading the Bible and the many stories of people who've gone through much worse ordeals than I have, that He has a purpose in allowing the troubles. He can use trials to strengthen our character, bring others to Him through how we handle our problems, or rely on Christ more. There could be a host of reasons, which I may never find out until Heaven.

Unfortunately, at times, I wasn't proud of how I acted. Sometimes I prayed, "God, would you just take me now. I'm ready to go to Heaven to be with you. I can't take this anymore." Oh, I would never act upon that thought myself, but the desire to leave this earth and the constant pain and go to Heaven definitely occurred during some of the extreme episodes.

When I read the Biblical story of the death of Lazarus, Martha and Mary's brother in John 11, I notice immediately that before Jesus raised their brother from the dead, He waited four days. I can imagine the joy Martha and Mary had upon seeing their brother alive on earth again. But I wondered why Jesus waited four days. I mean, He is God, He could have easily gotten there quicker, but He chose not to. He let Martha and Mary grieve over Lazarus during that time.

Again, because I'm not God, sometimes I don't see the answer, but I still have to believe in faith that God loved them and wanted to help, however He chose to. He showed that He alone controls the timing of Lazarus living again on earth, not Martha and Mary. When we can't control circumstances, we have to trust God and His reasons for doing or not doing something even when we desperately cry out to Him. The results of praying to Jesus aren't always like a microwave where we get the fastest results.

Ultimately, bringing Lazarus back from the dead, when He decided, brought the most glory to Christ. Oftentimes, trials involve suffering. "Not only so, but we also glory in our sufferings, because we know that suffering produces perseverance; perseverance, character; and character, hope. And hope does not put us to shame, because God's love has been poured out into our hearts through the Holy Spirit, who has been given to us" (Romans 5:3-5).

We have today. I don't know what the future holds or if my intestines will continue to be disease free. Naturally, I pray they do. But as the saying goes, I do know who holds the future in His hands. It's all about trusting in the King of glory—Jesus.

Note

A few years after being told of my no longer having Crohn's and ileocolitis, my primary doctor ordered another colonoscopy due to some anemia problems I experienced (from female issues). Dr. Grant performed the procedure and remembered me from seeing him several years before.

He said afterwards that everything was fine. I didn't need to return for another routine colonoscopy for ten years.

My friend Sue, who drove me to clinic for the test, later asked me when we she was driving me home. "Do you know what you did in the recovery room?"

"No, what do you mean?"

"You grabbed a tract from your purse and started sharing the Gospel with the doctor."

"I did?"

"Yes."

"And what did he say?" I asked her.

"He was listening."

I didn't remember that at all, but I pray one day, Dr. Grant will know Jesus as his Savior.

CHAPTER 30

The Nursing Home

"YOU WILL NEVER GET HIM to work with you." That's what I heard from my coworkers at the nursing home where I worked as a physical therapist.

"Why not?" I asked.

"He's just very stubborn and moody. We've tried multiple times to get him to try therapy and he just says 'no' or quits right after he starts."

"Well, I'm going to try anyway," I said.

As I exercised Tim, I found out by the age of forty-eight he had lived in different nursing homes for twenty-three years. He initially had an inoperable brain tumor, and then he suffered a subdural hematoma after that. He looked as though he had a stroke. Wheelchair bound, with right-sided weakness in his arm and leg, he had great difficulty speaking. I had to really listen to understand what Tim was trying to say, but even then I often had to ask him to repeat himself.

One of the first days I worked with Tim, I turned around briefly to assist another patient in the physical therapy gym. When I looked back, Tim had already wheeled himself out the door returning to his room.

"Tim!" I yelled, "Where are you going? We're not done yet!"

"I don't want to do therapy," he shouted back. He proceeded to wheel himself back to his room, using his arm on the hall railing and his left foot to propel himself.

I felt bad for him. Obviously younger than nearly all the other residents in the home, he had gone through a lot in his life. I thought the physical therapy could still help him, but he would need motivation to see any results.

A couple of times, I stopped by his room, just to say hi. Tim's sense of humor stood out when he was not in a bad mood over his disability and the fact that he lived in a nursing home. When Tim laughed, his chest and stomach bounced up and down. Over the next month, we became friends, and he started wheeling himself into therapy on his own.

Tim had much weakness. At 6'2", 220 pounds, and a lack of core stability, he was physically demanding to work with. Not to mention the mental challenges of needing to constantly encourage him to work hard. I often told jokes to try to lighten things up. It seemed to help.

After much effort, he managed to walk about ten feet using the hall railing while wearing a long leg brace. When Tim got fitted for the brace, I was in the room. He said to the brace man, "I like Pam because she loves Jesus." I felt honored by the statement.

I enjoyed talking to other residents, too. Noreen, a heavy woman with short white hair framing her face, porcelain-like skin and bright blue eyes, was wheelchair bound. I told Noreen her face reminded me of a china doll.

Noreen often asked me to come back to visit her in her room when I got off work. She had one daughter and some grandchildren who visited occasionally. As I sat next to the bed reading aloud to her, I saw their pictures on the wall in her room. We started in the book of John. Whenever I saw her again, whether it

Tim

was several days or a week or two later, she always knew exactly where we stopped reading.

"You were on John chapter 10," Noreen would say—or wherever I last read.

Good memory, I thought, much better than mine. She wept easily when I prayed with her for God to give her strength and joy. Each time as I prepared to leave the room, she'd say, "Pam, do you have to go? Stay!"

"I'll come back another time. I promise."

"Well, don't wait too long," she hollered from her bed, when previously her voice was soft spoken.

After working at this nursing home for three months, and with much difficulty, I resigned to take a different position. This proved an extremely difficult decision. Ironically, when I initially started working at the nursing home, I dreaded going to work. But by the time I quit, I had grown to love the people. Leaving resulted in a challenging transition, but mainly I chose to because of the heavy physical work.

On one of my last days, Tim wheeled down to the therapy gym.

"Tim," I said, "I'm going to miss everyone, including you. Maybe I can come back and visit sometime."

"You won't visit. People say that, but they never come back."

"Well, you'll have to wait and see. I bet I will."

What followed was seven years of visiting the residents every one to two months. Initially, I went by myself. But after

I mentioned to a few of my friends that I was going to visit the nursing home, especially friends from church, they shocked me and excitedly asked if they could come along with me.

We usually went on a Sunday afternoon, after our respective church services were over, and we met in the lobby of the nursing home. We had anywhere from a four to twenty people at a time. We knocked on the room doors of the residents' and if they invited us in, we'd visit. Sometimes, my friends Lynda and Laurie sang songs or we'd pray for the residents. My cousin Sandy and her daughter often took small gifts with Bible verses attached to give out. One of the men who came with us preached in the dining room on a few occasions. At several of these visits, I had the privilege of seeing residents repent of their sins and pray to trust in Jesus with their lives.

After a few hours, we'd meet back in the lobby. The amazing thing was we all seemed to enjoy the time that we gave to the residents, and they to us. Sometimes while driving there, my thoughts would go to…why am I doing this? Maybe this is just strange or crazy…visiting people in a nursing home so much. I wondered, 'Do they really enjoy our visits?' Until one day, I asked Tim, "Do you know when I was last here?"

"Six weeks ago," he said, "the middle of April, and before that the beginning of March."

That touched my heart. Wow, I thought, I can hardly believe he knew exactly when I was last here. Our visits do matter to him.

I also wondered if God wanted us to make these regular visits. Often I asked Him to make clear His will for my life. And He gave me this verse one day. "Be very careful, then, how you live—not as unwise but as wise, making the most of every opportunity, because the days are evil. Therefore do not be foolish, but understand what the Lord's will is" (Ephesians 5:15-17).

This confirmed that God really had his hand on this visitation

Lynda and Tim

ministry. I also knew that, throughout the Bible, God encourages us to take care of the orphans and widows—those who cannot take care of themselves.

From time to time, over the years, a few of us in the regular group who visited the nursing home would get emails from Tim. Usually, he just said 'hi' or asked us to bring him something. If we hadn't visited in more than a month, I almost always got an email. Everything he wrote was short and to the point; I'm sure it was difficult for Tim to type since he could use only one hand.

We decided to take Tim on an excursion one Sunday. We called the nursing desk ahead of time, so they knew we'd be taking him out for a few hours and they would have him ready to go. We loaded his wheelchair into the back of my SUV and transferred him to the front seat. Tim went to church with us that day followed by a stop at Applebee's Restaurant. They put several tables together at the restaurant to accommodate about fifteen people from our church to enjoy lunch together.

Other times over the years, we took Tim out and wheeled him around a boat harbor and the neighboring quaint shops. The outings for Tim seemed bittersweet. You could see Tim enjoyed himself, yet he knew he would return to the nursing home, so he often got very sad. He didn't like living there, and he complained frequently. His age, mental competence, and other factors made him dread it. He often said that he wanted his own apartment. I called the social work department and asked them about his situation. I knew that on occasion disabled people were able to have their own apartments with 24-hour care. Sadly, because I was not his power of attorney, I couldn't do much to change his situation.

It's hard to imagine someone living more than twenty-five years in a nursing home—bound in a wheelchair and barely able to make his needs known verbally. This nursing home was poorly cared for too. Tim's situation seemed extremely challenging.

I also could not change Tim's attitude. I often prayed and encouraged Tim to use the gifts God had given him perhaps to help or encourage others. Even his great sense of humor could be used for God's glory. "A cheerful heart makes merry medicine, but a downcast spirit dries up the bones" (Proverbs 17:22).

The apostles in the Bible are great examples I look to. When they were in prison, instead of constantly complaining about their situation, they sang songs and hymns to God and preached to the other prisoners about Jesus. I know they prayed a lot, too! They allowed God to use them for His Kingdom wherever they were.

Tim had a few living family members, but only one visited yearly. Bill, a previous neighbor from many years ago, spent time with Tim each month. One day when I came to see Tim, I saw that he had a nice, new TV, compliments of Bill. Eventually, however, Bill's job transferred him to another state and those visits stopped. I know Tim was sad about that.

Tim had been admitted to the hospital for short stays a few times since I had known him, usually for a problem with his diabetes. After his last hospitalization and returning to the nursing home, he started having issues with swallowing.

My friends, cousins, and I visited Tim frequently during that time. My friend Ana played the flute and her boyfriend played his guitar at Tim's bedside. During those few short weeks, Tim couldn't eat, and since he or his brother had signed a DNR (do not resuscitate) order, they didn't give him any IV's—just pain medications to make him as comfortable as possible. The week Tim died, a few of us sat with him nearly every day. We didn't want him to suffer alone. But Tim was never really alone; he loved Jesus, and He was with him through it all.

Knowing Tim made me realize the value of unconditional love. I learned the quality of friendship with another person who just like all the rest of us, has "issues." Remaining a friend to someone who couldn't pay me back in kind proved that a relationship—didn't have to be reciprocal. I experienced the truth that giving is better than receiving. And yet Tim gave to all of us something no one else could, his friendship. He is the person God made him to be, and, in spite of his physical challenges and emotional struggles, we all enjoyed his company.

Unfortunately, Noreen ended up having a double leg amputation due to poor circulation. About a year later, she went into eternity. I didn't know about her death until I went to visit her and the nursing staff told me she had passed away.

One day, I will see Tim and Noreen again, not disabled in wheelchairs, but in Heaven—healed with all the other followers of Jesus, praising Him for who He is and what He has done for us. It will be a celebration like no other.

Acknowledgements

IT HAS TAKEN MANY YEARS for these true stories contained within these pages to occur, as well as additional years for me to write and publish them. Though the journey has been long, the kingdom "work" has brought me joy and fulfillment.

First of all, I want to thank the Lord Jesus Christ. Without faith in Him, nothing is possible.

I want to thank the people I met and then wrote about in this book (most names have been changed). I hope our interactions blessed you as much as they did me. And for all those who encouraged, motivated, and helped me to get this book to print.

A huge thank you to the following: Northside Writers Group of Western New York, The Buffalo Writers Meetup Group, and Rockwall Christian Writers Group. I regularly attended those critique groups for years, and it's where I developed my writing "voice."

Heartfelt thanks to the many patients I've treated over the years as a physical therapist, many who read single chapters and asked me to put all the stories together into a book. As the patients returned for more stories, I realized my strong desire to inspire others to seek the Lord. One physical therapy patient told me she had so much anxiety, that for several days she slept with the chapters in her bed and would reread them for comfort.

Family and friends including Ana Entress, Israel Hernandez, Rob Stevens (who is now deceased), JoAnn LaMantia, and Mark and Jodi Weber have helped me greatly.

My editors Leslie Porter Wilson and Kathie Nee-Scriven, were wonderful to work with. They could see things that needed improvement as we all have blind spots. "Iron sharpens iron" (Proverbs 27:17).

My publishing coach, Kara Starcher of Mountain Creek Books, did a terrific job.

Makaira Todero is probably the number one supporter of *Bridge of Love*. I met her on social media through a mutual friend. Reading some of the stories I posted on Facebook sparked her curiosity about God—to the point she wanted to know Him. I continued to pray and talk with her. Within a few months, Makaira declared that she had become a Christian. This happened several years ago, and, although we have never met in person, we talk frequently. She must have asked me how my book was coming along nearly every single week since the beginning of this project, and she continued to insist I publish it as soon as possible.

I went on my first mission trip to Zambia, Africa, many years ago. At one of the conferences, I met a woman, Mutinta Mwanyanda who attended it. She is the founder of Salvation and Healing Ministries in Kabwe, Zambia. Through education, a feeding program, and a clinic, they help orphans and vulnerable children. A friend and mentor, she has offered me support and prayer from the start of this project to the finish.

I would also like to thank Sandy Flanigan, Dr. Hema Sakthivel, Lynda Hauser, Bill Marshall, and all the others who gave their input on my book.

I appreciate the many people who prayed for *Bridge of Love* to come to fruition and the many people involved who gave me advice and wisdom—a generous thank you!

About the Author—Pam's Story

MANY YEARS AGO, MY LIFE reflected a much different person than I am today. Five-six evenings of the week, I went out drinking with my friends, led a sexually immoral lifestyle, swore a lot, and had a huge anger problem. Basically, I believed—and acted like—the world revolved around me.

As a child, my family took me to a local church. I believed in the entities of God and Jesus, but I didn't see any relationship between Christ's death on the cross two thousand years ago and now.

Once on my own and out of my family's house, I stopped going to church except for Christmas and Easter. I went on those holidays only out of tradition, otherwise I saw no reason to go. Until one Sunday, I decided out of boredom and loneliness to look for a church. At the same time, I questioned in my mind what love really is, as I had gone through so many relationships with men. That uncertainty about unconditional love reminded me that I had received a Bible that I thought had "God is Love" printed on the cover. I found and decided to read that Bible—not a verse here and there as I had to memorize for confirmation—but really read it. I thought maybe it would tell me what love is.

Between searching for a church on Sundays and reading my Bible nearly every day, I realized that the Bible is a book all about love. Because of God's immense love for us, He wants us to live a certain way, to make wise decisions and abandon our sinful ways, and to be restored to a relationship with the Father through Jesus. He wants this just as a father who loves his child wants for that precious child of his.

I understood that going to Heaven is not based on anything we do (confirmation, baptism, selfless acts, etc.), but on what Jesus did on the cross. "We are saved by grace not works lest anyone should boast" (Ephesians 2:8-9). And Romans 3:23, which states: "The wages of sin is death but the gift of God is eternal life."

God gave me three gifts when I asked Him to forgive my sins and put my complete faith in Him. First, He gave me the opportunity to spend eternity in Heaven with Jesus. Second, He sent me the Holy Spirit as a helper, guide, and comforter here on earth. Third, the essence of my faith could be expressed in how I love Him and others.

Three months after I started searching for the meaning of love, I surrendered my life to Christ. Each day, I'm so grateful I made that life-changing decision in the fall of 1998. Obviously, I had not been living a Christian life. Ephesians 5:18 states "Don't be drunk with wine, because that will ruin your life. Instead, let the Holy Spirit fill and control you." I stopped getting drunk thinking that would make me happy. I also gave up my sexual immorality. "It is God's will that you should be sanctified:

that you should avoid sexual immorality" (1 Thessalonians 4:3). I abandoned both of these practices because I longed to please God—not out of obligation, but because I realized He has the best plan for me. To this day, He continues to refine me into His character for His glory. He's had a lot to work on.

God used my analytical nature—my deep desire to understand what love is—to look for Him, and I found love to *be* Him! Love is built upon a relationship with Jesus Christ. With this relationship, I now enjoy going to church and singing for Him; it's not forced or out of tradition.

As imperfect sinful beings—myself included—humans will fail us at times, but God's plans and His ways never fail because "love never fails" (1 Corinthians 13:8).

Over the years, God has changed me in many ways and will continue to do so until the day I die (He does this to all followers of Christ). We call this process sanctification. The person I used to be—the drinking, foul-mouthed, short-tempered person who led an immoral lifestyle—is not the person I am today (2 Corinthians 5:17). Nor would I have been inspired to do things as Jesus would—go on mission trips, teach Bible studies, give money sacrificially, and serve others who couldn't pay me back. I did these things, only because of Jesus, only because of Him.

No amount of discipline or physical training can change the inner heart and mind into a person who loves and surrenders their life to Jesus. As you read this book, you've seen many of my conversations occurred with people of other beliefs. The difference between Christianity and all the other religions in the world is that the Christian God is alive and wants a relationship with you, now and forever.

If you read this book and you already have surrendered your life to Christ, live for Him. "But you will receive power when the Holy Spirit comes on you; and you will be my witnesses in

Jerusalem, and in all Judea and Samaria, and to the ends of the earth" (Acts 1:8). He's a living God, the only one, and the whole earth needs Him.

Five Lessons I've Learned
During Sickness or Going Through a Trial

OVER THE YEARS, I'VE LEARNED some lessons during the difficult times in my life. I've included them here:

1. Make God your "refuge and strength, an ever-present help in trouble" (Psalm 46:1). Even though God often uses other people in our lives to help us, seek Him first in all areas of your life.

   Pray to the Lord for help. Also give others your prayer requests including your church. The Bible says, "Do not be anxious about anything, but in every situation, by prayer and petition, with thanksgiving, present your requests to God. And the peace of God, which transcends all understanding, will guard your hearts and your minds in Christ Jesus" (Philippians 4:6-7). Oftentimes, prayers are not answered immediately, but give Him time. Prayer requires patience. His answer may be yes, no, or not now.

2. Be willing to reach out to others for assistance. I encourage you to share your prayer requests with others, including your

church family. Also, depending on the problem, getting help quickly could be critical as some things require immediate attention. Go to your doctor, family, and friends. Sometimes issues will only get bigger if you don't seek appropriate assistance. Remember, God often uses other people in our lives. We are interdependent on one another.

Choose to reach out to others who will inspire and help you, those you can confide in. It's important to be authentic and transparent with supportive, trustworthy, godly people. Having family and friends who encourage you is a blessing, but not everyone responds to adversity with understanding and compassion. So let others know your needs and what you are going through. But remember, those family members and friends are not your Savior, only Jesus can be. Don't rely solely on one person. Over time chronic neediness can challenge a good relationship.

When going through a tough situation, try to make sure the relationship goes both ways. Sincerely ask about the other person's life; find out what they're going through. Be a giver, not just a taker—both relationally and materially. With kindness and compassion, through prayer, and by what you have the ability to offer another person, you can bless someone else in the midst of your own trial.

Sometimes having a godly counselor or mentor helps you to see things from a different perspective and process a situation. "Plans fail for lack of counsel, but with many advisers they succeed" (Proverbs 15:22).

3. Listen to Christian praise music. The words and melodies will soothe your burdened soul. It's also a motivator that will help get your mind off your problem and onto God and others. We see this very thing in Scripture. When the disciples were

in prison they sang to the Lord. "About midnight Paul and Silas were praying and singing hymns to God, and the other prisoners were listening to them" (Acts 16:25).

Perhaps, at times, the disciples felt discouraged and experienced much pain. They were human, but they kept their focus on Christ. They used their gifts for God's glory, sharing the Gospel—even while in prison and probably in pain. Their circumstances were not ideal, so do not always expect yours to be either. God can use you wherever you are in life, and He can use whatever you're going through to bring glory to Him and make Himself known to others.

4. Thank God by having an attitude of gratitude. There is so much to be thankful for, even if it's "just" having a bed to sleep on, air to breathe, food to eat. And we should definitely be grateful for our salvation.

   The Bible says when we go through trials, and we all do, they build up our faith. "Consider it pure joy, my brothers and sisters, whenever you face trials of many kinds, because you know that the testing of your faith produces perseverance. Let perseverance finish its work so that you may be mature and complete, not lacking anything" (James 1:2-4). We may not enjoy what's happening—that's why it's called a trial—but we can thank God for helping us through it.

5. Do what you can—even though you may have a disability or illness. A follower of Christ is in a transformation process throughout their life, with the ultimate goal of becoming more like Jesus. No one is perfect. He simply wants you to recognize His sovereignty and lordship and use your gifts and talents to serve Him and tell others about Him as you are able.

   Try to enjoy life, too. "Command those who are rich in this present world not to be arrogant nor to put their hope in wealth, which is so uncertain, but to put their hope in God, who richly provides us with everything for our enjoyment" (1 Timothy 6:17).

What I've Learned about Sharing the Gospel

1. Share the Gospel out of a motivation of love. Jesus' death on the cross—His willing sacrifice for you and me—showed His incredible generosity towards sinners. Think about a person becoming a believer perhaps because of seeds of the Gospel that you planted. Wouldn't that be amazing, the best thing you could ever hope for? When you love someone, you want the best for them. The best decision is to trust in Jesus. "For God so loved the world that He gave His one and only Son, that whoever believes in Him shall not perish but have eternal life" (John 3:16). Think about what it would mean for them to come to know Jesus Christ and follow Him on Earth, so that you will eventually see them in Heaven one day. What a marvelous reunion!

   The consequence for refusing to believe in Christ as Savior is to spend eternity in Hell—an unremitting, terrible place. I wouldn't want anyone to go there.

2. Don't be overly concerned with saying exactly the "right words" to share Christ. The Holy Spirit will help you to share the Gospel, and in time it will get easier. It's kind of like riding a bike; the first time is always difficult. But don't let fear stop you.

God will use you where you are. You can tell the unbeliever the story of how Christ has changed you, even if you are a new Christian. You can share with them why we all have a need for Him. You can always bridge the conversation from the natural—talking about family, friends, hobbies, or work, and then shifting to spiritual things.

3. Read your Bible. Get into Bible studies and small groups where you can understand particularly harder Biblical passages with other believers. "Do your best to present yourself to God as one approved, a worker who does not need to be ashamed and who correctly handles the word of truth" (2 Timothy 2:15).

   You don't need to know everything if questions come up. If you don't know an answer to someone's question, tell them you will look into that and get back to them. You can also refer a person to a local church near where they live, or point them to a Christian website that might help them, such as gotquestions.org, livingwaters.com, carm.org, or another good apologetics website.

4. Encourage the person to seek God through reading the Bible, especially the Gospels—Matthew, Mark, Luke, and John. If they don't have a Bible, perhaps offer to get them one. Follow through on any promises you make, too. I gave a co-worker a Bible once and forgot that I had given him one. Years later, he told me he'd read some of it. That encouraged me. "So is my word that goes out from my mouth: It will not return to me empty, but will accomplish what I desire and achieve the purpose for which I sent it" (Isaiah 55:11).

   Many websites offer free pamphlets that you can print out regarding having a relationship with Jesus. You can also purchase Bibles, New Testaments, or the book of John fairly inexpensively through many ministries. Many people now download the Bible onto their phone. I still prefer a tangible paper copy to look at generally.

5. Pray for boldness in sharing the Gospel and open doors where people are responding to your sharing Jesus with them. Pray for people's hearts to be softened—rather than hardened. We don't know how God will use what we have said and done for others, so prayerfully ask the Lord for opportunities and ideas. It's a privilege to share the Gospel. You are then a co-laborer with Jesus for the Kingdom of God.

   Often a spiritual conversation will not happen, unless we swing the conversation in that direction. That's what Jesus did. He started in the natural and moved the conversation to the spiritual. For example, think about Jesus' interaction with the woman at the well in John 4. That can happen by bringing something up in your own life or asking the person a question. For instance, ask what they did over the weekend? If they don't mention going to church, you could remark that you really enjoyed the church service you went to and then ask if they attend a church.

6. Consider giving financially to ministries that share the Gospel—especially those in countries where Christianity is illegal. Many ministries allow you to donate to give Bibles overseas. Others accept donations to help support evangelists who share the Good News. Many people do not have the opportunities that we have in the United States to go to church, own a Bible, and hear about Jesus.

   Consider verifying the trustworthiness of the ministry by checking their financial accountability to ensure they are using contributions wisely. Unfortunately, some "ministries" have been known to deceive people for their money.

One time, I planned to do a bike ride to support a local secular charity. My friend Jane, (chapter 25), became upset when a mutual friend wanted to donate a small amount of money to me. Jane said, "It would be better to give the money to those who directly share the Gospel. Non-Christians can donate to secular causes."

At first, I didn't agree with her. But the more I thought about it, I realized she did have a point. Sharing the Gospel is most important. We all have to decide for ourselves where to steward our money.

Do you really need that extra sweater, or trinket? People overseas, including children, are dying every day from hunger, poor or no healthcare, or a lack of water. And very importantly, over a billion people have not heard the Gospel. These are needs that we can meet, real needs believers can help with. Let's be the hands, feet, and mouth of Jesus.

How to Have a Relationship with Jesus

AS HUMANS, WE ARE ALL sinners. "For all have sinned and fallen short of the glory of God" (Romans 3:23). Because of our fallen, sinful nature, we deserve death. We will all physically die one day and stand before the judgment seat of Christ where we will be judged for "every secret thing, whether good or evil" (Ecclesiastes 12:14).

If you have lied, lusted, taken the Lord's name in vain, hated another, you will be found guilty on Judgment Day. (See Exodus 20, the Ten Commandments.) Without exception, we are all sinners.

You will suffer the judgment for your sins for all eternity in Hell—a horrible place. Yet, because of God's immense love and mercy, He sent Jesus, the Savior who died on the cross to take the punishment for our sins so that we can be forgiven and spend eternity in Heaven with Him.

"For God so loved the world that He gave His one and only Son, that whoever believes in Him shall not perish but have eternal life" (John 3:16).

Repent and place your trust in Jesus for your salvation. The moment you trust in Him as your Lord and Savior, you will receive the Holy Spirit who will live with you forever (Ephesians 1:13). What a blessing this promise is! The Holy Spirit will help you while on earth. And, after you die, you will spend eternity in Heaven.

Read your Bible daily, and obey it. Find a good Bible-believing church to attend. You will grow in your relationship with Him, the best love and friend you can ever have.

None of us knows when we will take our last breath. Seek God, and believe in Jesus as your Lord and Savior, before it's too late.

Epilogue & Challenge

PRIOR TO MY BECOMING A follower of Jesus, I had a strong desire to attend parties where there were lots of people and often much drinking. The Lord has changed me so much that now I want to celebrate Him, and I want people to be filled with the Holy Spirit instead of alcohol (Ephesians 5:18).

One of my favorite verses is, "There is rejoicing in the presence of the angels of God over one sinner who repents" (Luke 15:10). Imagine the celebration in Heaven when we finally see Jesus and all other believers!

I want as many people as possible to go to Heaven—and avoid the devastation of Hell, don't you? So live for Jesus, and share the Gospel with a dying world desperately in need of Him.

IF ANYONE WOULD LIKE TO donate to the Zambia, Africa, charities I reference in my stories, here is their contact information:

Bana Besu Feeding Project and Lufutuko Community School

Facebook: Bana Besu Feeding Project or Lufutuko Community School and Bana Besu Feeding project

Any further questions: Mutinta Mwananyanda at shministries2003@gmail.com

The PET Project

Facebook: PET Zambia

Websites: PetZambia.org, www.NewLifeZambia.org

Any further questions: Delbert & Sandy Groves at groves@newlifezambia.com